TAKE STOCK

INNOVATION

COLLECTION

Take Stock in
Children®

ISBN 978-1-54396-934-4 eBook 978-1-54396-935-1

INTRODUCTION

Take Stock in Children is a non-profit organization serving the state of Florida that offers students a way out of poverty and into higher education through scholarships, mentors, and hope. The organization was founded in 1995 by a group of education, community, and business leaders frustrated by the large number of at-risk children in Florida not accessing higher education and being shut out of life-changing jobs and opportunities. Together, they created a simple, yet transformative solution. Students are recruited in middle and high school and receive comprehensive support through post-secondary graduation. Each student benefits from weekly meetings with a volunteer adult mentor, professional post-secondary success and career coaching, and sign a contract agreeing to remain drug and crime free and maintain high attendance and grades. In exchange for this commitment students receive a post-secondary scholarship to mitigate the financial barrier to higher education.

Take Stock in Children has served over 32,000 students during its 24-year history and has produced remarkable results:

96% of Take Stock in Children students graduate high school on time

92% of Take Stock in Children students enter post-secondary education

68% of Take Stock in Children students complete post-secondary education, compared to the state average of 27% for at-risk students in poverty

Developing the Take Stock Innovation Collection

In 2015, Take Stock in Children was awarded an Investing in Innovation (i3) federal grant from the US Department of Education. The UNISON project (Uplifting Non-cognitive Skills and Innovation through Student Opportunity Networks) improved student outcomes in low-performing schools and piloted service innovations with the potential to impact the entire Take Stock in Children network, comprised of more than 8,000 students. The i3 grant program is focused on bringing innovations to scale; therefore, a specific methodology was followed to develop each of the six elements of the Take Stock Innovation Collection. First, the UNISON scaling team began by codifying the models implemented during the grant. This was accomplished by conducting interviews, document reviews, and field research. Next, select Take Stock in Children affiliates were invited to review and test the innovations and their materials. Finally, all affiliate feedback was incorporated into the models. Based on the findings from the field tests, this supporting manual was created and made available to every Take Stock in Children affiliate.

This edition presents six specific elements of the Take Stock Innovation Collection. They include Collective Impact, Alternative Financial Aid Models, the School-Based Approach, Post-Secondary Partnerships, Group Mentoring, and Virtual Mentoring

1. Collective Impact Approach – Collective Impact is a strategy that can magnify growth by aligning partners to resourcefully implement services that progress toward a common goal. This strategy goes beyond traditional coordinated efforts and is particularly defined by the presence of a strong infrastructure, common agenda, and commitment to measurement. This is especially important in a school environment where multiple partners with various goals may be working with the same students. This approach is found effective across sectors, including education, health, business, and agriculture.

2. Financial Aid & Alternative Scholarship Models – The financial barrier to college is one of the greatest challenges that at-risk students and their families face when it comes to post-secondary access and completion. A key feature of the Take Stock in Children model is to provide a Florida Prepaid Scholarship to each student enrolled in the program. While this will remain the central feature of the model, UNISON, Upward Bound, and other projects have identified the opportunity to serve a greater number of students via alternative strategies, such as intensive financial aid counseling and support. Ideas like "last dollar in" scholarships have also proved an impactful solution. Additionally, affiliates have experienced success with helping students access early college and other programs that offer post-secondary credit in high school.

3. School-Based Approach – The school-based approach is also a strategy that can be used to accelerate program growth and impact by pooling resources to maximize service level efficiency. This approach is particularly effective in schools attended by larger numbers of Take Stock in Children students.

4. Post-Secondary Partnership Approach – Partnering with post-secondary institutions can also extend Take Stock in Children's impact by better equipping students for their post-secondary experience. It is a mutually beneficial strategy, which also serves colleges' and universities' goals to recruit and retain students. This strategy can be implemented along a continuum, ranging from informal partnerships based on individual relationships to codified agreements with shared staffing.

5. Group Mentoring – The overall success of Take Stock in Children along with the increasing number of at-risk students highlight the need to continue to grow the number of students served across the organization. However, this growth also presents challenges, especially with regard to finding the number of mentors needed to serve the increasing population of students. Group-oriented mentoring empowers students to become advocates for their success by sharing information and offering advice, social support, coaching, and counseling.

6. Virtual Mentoring – Virtual mentoring is an approach that can efficiently and effectively result in greater numbers of students served by mentors. Virtual mentoring is for participants who rely on electronic tools to communicate for some meetings and is utilized as a supplement to in-person mentoring sessions.

Take Stock in Children would like to thank the Helios Education Foundation, TIAA Bank, and the US Department of Education for supporting the UNISON project and for making the Take Stock Innovation Collection possible

Take Stock Innovation Collection: Collective Impact Approach

Take Stock in Children®

The contents of this manual were developed under a grant from the U.S. Department of Education, Investing in Innovation (i3) Program. However, those contents do not necessarily represent the policy of the U.S. Department of Education, and you should not assume endorsement by the federal government.

Table of Contents

ACKNOWLEDGEMENTS

Take Stock in Children would like to thank and acknowledge the UNISON team, who has tirelessly worked to launch and successfully implement the innovations supported by Take Stock in Children's Investing in Innovation (i3) grant. This team, led by Judy Saylor, Director of Program Growth and Innovation, includes Tiara Arline, Sara Buckley, Tiffany Givens, Amy Grunder, Roxanne Jordan, and Luz Rodriguez. The i3 grant program is ultimately about reaching scale — taking innovations from pilot to multiple sites and programs. Through the hard work of this team, these innovations will impact over 8,500 students per year through 45 independent affiliates across the Take Stock in Children network.

Finally, Take Stock in Children would like to recognize Gary Romano and the Civitas Strategies team for guiding the codification and scaling process of the innovations developed during the i3 grant program.

The increased number of students served along with a continually growing demand means that the UNISON innovations will provide the network with opportunities to efficiently use resources as well as maintain a high level of programmatic quality and service delivery. Scaling these elements will not only benefit the Take Stock in Children network but will also accelerate the progress of national scaling efforts. Network-wide adoption will effectively result in additional proof points and data, all which will contribute to a climate conducive to national uptake.

Introduction

The Take Stock in Children (TSIC) model of support is built upon the positive relationships that students develop with their mentors. The impact that a caring adult can have on a student's academic and social-emotional development has been proven in field-based research. Strong evidence suggests that a community-based mentoring approach decreases drug and alcohol use, enhances peer and parent-child relationships, increases school attendance, and improves attitudes about and performance in school (Tierney, Grossman and Resch, 1995).

These positive outcomes are also illustrated in the outstanding results of TSIC students. Each TSIC student is matched with a caring adult mentor who meets with the student at his/her school for an hour each week.

Mentors provide academic and behavioral motivation, guidance, friendship, and support. This effective mentor support has greatly contributed to Take Stock in Children's results:

96% of Take Stock in Children students graduate high school on time

92% of Take Stock in Children students enter post-secondary education

68% of The Stock in Children Students complete post-secondary education, compared to the state average of 27% for at-risk students in poverty

The overall success of the program along with the increasing number of students in need has encouraged affiliates to target growth in an effort to increase the number of students served across the organization.

Collective Impact is a strategy that can magnify growth by aligning partners to implement services efficiently and effectively. This strategy goes beyond traditional coordinated efforts and is particularly defined by the presence of a strong infrastructure, common agenda, and commitment to measurement. This is especially important in a school environment where multiple partners with parallel goals may be working with the same students. The approach is found effective across sectors, including education, health, business, and agriculture.

The TSIC Collective Impact Model is a strategy developed through its UNISON project, a federally funded Investing in Innovation (i3) grant implemented at three school sites where collective impact was integrated into the implementation. The lessons learned from this project were instrumental in codifying the model for replication across the network.

This section of the Take Stock Innovation Collection is the result of that codification and presents the information you need to launch and implement the TSIC Collective Impact Model.

Material covered in this manual includes the following:

- The definition of Collective Impact
- When to use Collective Impact
- The benefits of Collective Impact
- The challenges of Collective Impact and how to address them
- Strategies for Collective Impact, including creating a team, designing and executing an action plan, and communicating for success
- Tools for Collective Impact implementation

The launching of any new program can be challenging, regardless of the depth of the instructions. If you have any questions not covered in the manual or feedback in general you would like to share, please contact the Take Stock in Children State Office.

From The Front Lines

As part of the data collection for this manual's development, we interviewed staff who led the pilot Collective Impact approach. Throughout this manual, you will find some of the wisdom gathered and lessons learned from their experience with the implementation process; these unique insights are located in subtext like this one, titled "From the Front Lines.

CHAPTER (1) Why Collective Impact?

Definition

In an attempt to meet school turnaround objectives and effect positive change, low-performing schools are continually shifting and changing as new interventions and programming are introduced. This occurs both internally (with district policies and staff) and externally (with community-based organizations).

Having an array of community-based organizations operating within schools can provide many students with much needed services such as mental health, tutoring, mentoring, after-school activities, etc. To effectively serve students, the school staff must understand the services, staffing model, and student selection process of each organization.

The need to create a strategy for communication and coordination of efforts also proves critical. This helps avoid a negative culture that includes competing interests, distrust, overlapping of services, and lack of awareness among school staff, all of which can diminish this important work's impact. Collective Impact is one such strategy that can serve to align partners around shared goals and coordinated services.

Five Characteristics of Collective Impact

- ✓ Common agenda
- ✓ Shared measurement system
- ✓ Mutually reinforcing activities
- ✓ Continuous communication
- ✓ Backbone organization

Five Benefits of Collective Impact

In addition to Collective Impact encompassing five key characteristics as listed above, sites that have piloted the Collective Impact approach have reported five vital benefits:

1. Perspective-Taking – The Collective Impact approach provides a venue for schools and partners to communicate clearly about the school landscape, assets, and unmet needs.

2. Developing Common Language – All team members access the common knowledge and information sharing that contributes to a joint understanding of current students' needs as well as factors that impact success across all service providers.

3. Understanding Challenges – Team meetings give space and tools to identify barriers to success. This identification process is the first step to creating a plan that mitigates these challenges.

4. Setting Common Goals – The Collective Impact approach helps partners make sure they are working toward the same ultimate outcomes

5. Timely Action – A core component of Collective Impact lies in not only identifying resources and needs but also creating an action plan to pursue common goals. This plan is executed and refined consistently, using regular meetings to maintain communication.

Challenges of Collective Impact

Collective Impact may be an unfamiliar approach and can present certain challenges.

First, it requires a shift from "business as usual," primarily in moving outside of silos to truly collaborate with others. This can be particularly challenging for organizations with limited resources and staffing. Collective Impact work calls for ongoing communication, often especially hard for those with already high demands on their time

Second, some teams may find it difficult to define a common goal. This is due to traditionally isolated work, distrust of others, or the lack of incentives to collaborate (National Governors Association, 2014). Funding streams might de-incentivize collaboration as individual organizations are funded to achieve certain goals independently

Third, rurally-located affiliates might find this approach more challenging than do urban programs. Urban TSIC affiliates likely have a greater number of potential partner organizations to work with and may find geographic proximity helpful in terms of holding in-person meetings. However, due to the benefits and potential outcomes associated with Collective Impact initiatives, rural affiliates may still find a great advantage in exploring the use of this model.

Finally, some people we interviewed for this manual's development noted that while the benefits of Collective Impact may be great, the logistics of starting and sustaining an effective initiative can be quite challenging. Interviewees emphasized that it can be all too easy to take on too many partners or set too many initial goals during the start-up phase; you will find that this manual discusses this in great detail. Note that when you are determining whether a Collective Impact initiative is right for your affiliate, starting small and expanding the project slowly proves critical. In this way, you ensure that decisions made and steps taken are sustainable, given time and resource capacity.

From the Front Lines

➤ The goal of a Collective Impact partnership should always be to maximize existing and potential resources to most effectively address the cognitive, academic, and social-emotional needs of the students you serve.

➤ When weighing the benefits and challenges of implementing CI, the pilot team found it critical to consider what realistic outcomes were feasible to achieve.

➤ Further, they spent substantial time discussing whether the identified outcomes were worth the significant time/energy investment required to achieve their goals.

➤ One question they considered was whether pre-existing supports were in place to help facilitate implementation and make their goals more feasible.

➤ For example, they identified the external organizations that team members already had working relationships with, which helped expedite the CI development process

CHAPTER 2 Research

Collective Impact was highlighted in the *Stanford Social Innovation Review in Winter* 2011, which differentiates the approach from typical collaboration:

> "Unlike most collaborations, Collective Impact initiatives involve a centralized infrastructure, a dedicated staff, and a structured process that leads to a common agenda, shared measurement, continuous communication, and mutually reinforcing activities among all participants"[1]

Collective Impact is the opposite of isolated impact, which is defined as "an approach oriented toward finding and funding a solution embodied within a single organization, combined with the hope that the most effective organizations will grow or replicate to extend their impact more widely."

The report cites successful projects in education, the environment, public health, and agriculture. In Cincinnati, Ohio, a non-profit called Strive has convened local leaders to address student achievement and improve education across greater Cincinnati and Northern Kentucky.

Since 2007, they have seen the following impact:

> "86 percent of student outcome indicators are improving for students in Cincinnati and Northern Kentucky; third-grade reading achievement for Cincinnati Public School students is at 73 percent; and high school graduation rates for [students in]

both Covington Independent Public Schools and Newport Independent Schools are over 90 percent" (www.strivetogether.org).

The Strive model is being replicated nationally, with other regions experiencing similar success.

Shape Up Somerville is a citywide effort in Somerville, Massachusetts, designed to reduce and prevent obesity among elementary school children. In this cross-sector initiative, with Tufts University playing a leadership role, schools, local restaurants, and the local government each took actions that encouraged healthy eating and increased physical activity. Evaluation showed a statistically significant decrease in BMI score (Stanford, 2011).

---

1 J. Kamia and M. Kramer, "Collective Impact," Stanford Social Innovation Review, (2011, Winter), 36-41.

**Research defines five key conditions for
Collective Impact (FSG, 2011)**

1. **Common Agenda:** All participants have a shared vision for change, including an understanding of the problem and how to address it.

2. **Shared Measurement:** Participants collect and analyze data consistently, working toward common metrics.

3. **Mutually Reinforcing Activities:** Activities are differentiated and coordinated, with a specific plan of action.

4. **Continuous Communication:** Consistent communication across partners helps build trust and stay aligned with mutual objectives.

5. **Backbone Organization:** A separate organization with staff and specific skills coordinates the initiative as well as other organizations.

CHAPTER (3) Launching Collective Impact

Overview of Collective Impact Implementation

Three steps are critical for launching and maintaining a Collective Impact project. These are discussed in detail in the following sections. Please note, the affiliate staff interviewed in the development of this manual noted that Collective Impact is a complex process and should be implemented thoughtfully and with deliberation. The process outlined in this session should be considered a long-term approach, with a robust timeline allocated for implementation.

1. Assess Landscape

2. Design Action Plan

3. Execute and Refine Plan

Step 1: Assess the Landscape

The first step toward a successful Collective Impact project is to understand the current landscape of resources and partners by using information gathered through research, interviews, and group discussions (Take Stock in Children, 2015). You will want to consider multiple data sources, including qualitative and quantitative data on the community you are looking to serve. Sources for quantitative data might include recent census data or information from the Department of Education website. To collect qualitative data, we recommend conducting a series of interviews with relevant stakeholders: students, parents, school personnel, community leaders, and service providers. Some of the questions to consider include the following:

- What organizations and agencies are currently providing services to students in the targeted school(s)?
- What organizations are currently providing services to students in the community?
- What are the greatest unmet needs of students at the targeted school (academic, cognitive, social-emotional, behavioral, etc.)?
- What are the demographics of students' families?
- What are the current high school graduation and college attendance rates?
- What are the issues currently impacting these rates?
- What post-secondary programs are students most likely to attend?
- What could be done with existing resources to fill service gaps?

- What collaborative efforts were undertaken in the past and why were they successful/not successful?

Expert Tip

When assessing the landscape, consider what is realistic given the resources already in place.

For example, does your team already have existing relationships with some of the organizations you are considering partnering with? Does your TSIC model include a staff member embedded at your target school(s) who could serve as the point person for a collective action initiative?

A full assessment of the resources you have at the ready will be helpful further down the line when establishing team goals that are both ambitious and realistic. You may find that prerequisite steps would be helpful to take before attempting to tackle Collective Impact.

On the flipside, you may find that you are actually already doing some Collective Impact work with existing partners, just not labeling it as such. In this case, consider who else could be brought to the collective table to further support these efforts, rather than starting from scratch with a new goal.

Also, Collective Impact veterans consistently noted the importance of developing the project slowly so that your efforts are sustainable. It is easy to feel that the more partners involved the better, but the larger the scale the more overwhelming the logistics of managing the program can become.

It is okay—and in fact, preferable—to start small; 1-2 working partnerships can have impact, and there is always the possibility of further expansion once the initial project is off the ground!

Identifying Potential Partners

The primary goal of assessing the landscape is to gather as much information as possible about what opportunities and challenges currently exist and how these might have been previously addressed over time. As noted, both interviews and group meetings will be effective strategies for learning this information. Remember to always ask who else should be included as this is an important technique for identifying unlikely partners.

The first partner to consider should generally be the local school district. If the district or system you work with has a Community Engagement officer or department, they should be your first point of contact as there may already be a Collective Impact initiative (whether formal or informal) occurring.

Other example partner organizations include the local public school system; Big Brothers, Big Sisters (or other local mentoring programs); local colleges and universities and nonprofits working toward college completion rates; tutoring programs; relevant afterschool and summer programs; SAT/ACT prep organizations; homeless shelters with a TSIC-eligible student population; drug and alcohol awareness organizations; mental health advocates; relevant government agencies; and local and regional philanthropy organizations and leadership councils.

From the Front Lines

When identifying potential partners, make sure to consider possibilities outside of the school, especially if the school doesn't have many external partnerships already in place. For example, if the desired outcome of the Collective Impact initiative is to increase post-secondary attendance, it would be highly important to include representatives from local campuses and programs, as well as any organizations committed to college readiness. Make sure to ask potential partners for their recommendations as well—they may have working relationships formed with potential partners you weren't aware of.

EXERCISE 1: Identify and Interview Partners

1) Create a list of all the partners in the participating schools:

   a) Start with the partners you know.

   b) Make sure to include relevant district staff.

   c) Ask stakeholders who else should be included in these conversations.

2) Add potential partners from within the community to your list.

3) Craft a communication to the desired partners to gauge interest.

4) Once a final list is created, interview each partner. See **Attachment A** for suggested questions.

5) Identify each partner's goals, strengths, and challenges. Develop an understanding of the constituents they currently serve.

Use the template in Attachment B to organize information about the partners identified.

Correlate and Organize Information

Once you have gathered the partner information, you will need to make sense of how the data will impact your vision for a Collective Impact initiative. First, you will need to summarize each of the partner programs. Then you can identify common goals and challenges as well as opportunities that may be addressed together. Exercise 2, listed below, can help with this task.

EXERCISE 2: Identify Common Goals and Challenges

Use the chart you developed in **Attachment B** to create a series of lists:

1) Common goals

2) Common challenges

3) Common ideas of unmet needs

4) Common identification of successes / met needs

5) Opportunities for alignment of activities

Looking at the information from all partners collectively will provide a bird's-eye view that will be unique and provide a critical starting point for the next phase of work.

Set an Agenda

Your partners have shared important information with you, and now it is time to share with them what you have learned.

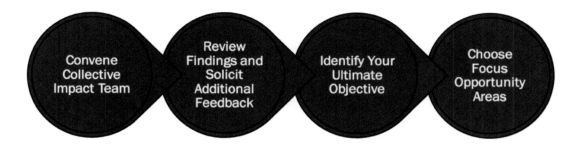

From the Front Lines

When going through their goal-setting process, the pilot team found it useful to create a collective list of all the challenges the partner organizations face in achieving their goals. Then they identified the challenges they experienced in common—for example, lack of parent involvement and consistent data sharing—then built their collective action goals around addressing these obstacles. The team also looked for ways to align goals with the target school's district-mandated improvement plan, which helped elicit buy-in from school personnel and further align collective efforts

First, decide who should be on your Collective Impact Team (CIT). Members of your team should be those who understand the landscape and opportunities for growth, provide services to the student population, and can collaborate to have a broad and deep impact.

Second, convene a meeting (or a series of meetings) with your team. At this meeting:

1) Review your findings about the landscape, including barriers, successes, opportunities, and partners. Confirm that what you have observed is aligned with partners' experiences, and add any additional information. Leave space for discussion and reflection to help build partner buy-in.

2) As a group, identify your key objectives for student impact. What change does your team hope to effect? It is critical that you narrow this down, as you can't do everything at once!

3) Identify related opportunities to pursue. What will you do in order to reach your goals? Your list of potential opportunities may be long. The success of your project hinges on buy-in from the Collective Impact Team about which ones you will pursue together; therefore, it proves important to share the list you have developed and ask if anything is missing. Then, as a group, determine what will be the top 3-5 priorities for which you will develop an action plan.

Sample objectives for a Collective Impact plan might include:

✓ Increase the number of high school graduates.

✓ Increase the number of students continuing to higher education.

✓ Increase the number of students enrolled in Advanced Placement classes.

✓ Increase student engagement in instructional activities.

✓ *Project objectives should be SMART goals – Specific, Measurable, Attainable, Realistic, and Timebound.*

BEST PRACTICES FOR IDENTIFYING PRIORITIES

✓ Align with the school improvement plan for maximum buy-in.

✓ Align with SMART goals (see list above)

Consider which opportunities can have an outsized impact on students

EXERCISE 3: Narrow Down Your List of Collective Impact Opportunities

Write all of the opportunities you have identified—and any others that the group adds—on chart paper or a white board.

1) Give each participant 3-5* stickers (foil stars or colored dots work well).

2) Ask each participant to place their stickers next to their top choices for opportunities to focus on as a Collective Impact Team. Remind the group that this is your first set of goals; you may return to this list to identify other priorities in the future.

3) Tally the stickers—the opportunities with the most stickers become your focus.

4) If there are no obvious "winners," do two rounds. After the first round, give just 5-7 choices and vote again.

Step 2: Design an Action Plan

Now that you have a team and have identified your priority opportunities, your next step is to create an action plan so these ideas can become a reality and make an impact on your students' outcomes. To be successful, implement the following steps:

♦ Set a Meeting Schedule for Partners

Consistency and communication are keys for success; therefore, it is important to set a regular meeting schedule for the whole group. Once a regular meeting schedule has been established, create a shared Google calendar to track these and other activities. The Collective Impact Coordinator will plan and facilitate these meetings with input from the larger group.

♦ Outline Roles and Responsibilities of Partners

Clarify expectations including attendance at meetings, leadership on various activities, and channels for communication. As part of this process, you will need to identify who will serve as the Collective Impact Coordinator

One of the consistent success factors for Collective Impact projects is having a backbone organization, with resources allocated toward coordinating efforts and maintaining partner organizations' momentum. For example, Take Stock in Children's UNISON project has incorporated a full-time coordinator for each project, although this also could be one part of someone's larger role.

Responsibilities include:

- Leading, planning, and supporting partners.

- Facilitating team planning.
- Providing logistical and administrative support.

Key Qualities of a Collective Impact Coordinator

✓ Strong organizational skills

✓ Clear communicator

✓ Relationship builder

✓ Experienced meeting facilitator

Hiring the coordinator (or creating space for an existing staff member to manage the project) will help keep the Collective Impact work on track and put ideas into action. The following steps will be largely coordinated and facilitated by the Collective Impact Coordinator with support from his/her organization (the backbone agency). Affiliates noted that some school districts might be able/willing to appoint district personnel to serve in this capacity.

When developing the work plan, the pilot team aimed to build a comprehensive outline of how they planned to achieve each established goal. For example, for each opportunity, the team identified a detailed SMART goal statement—a sequential list of tasks needed to accomplish the goal, helpful resources and supports, any relevant deadlines, clearly defined measure(s) of success, and the person/org. responsible for facilitating

Expert Tip:

The effort required to coordinate a Collective Impact project can be extensive. If you are planning to use an affiliate staff member as the Collective Impact Coordinator, it is most effective to use an individual already embedded into the school. Embedded TSIC

staff members will already have strong working relationships with school personnel as well as a working knowledge of the service providers and external partners already established. They are also more likely to have the capacity to add this role to their current responsibilities if they aren't currently traveling between multiple locations.

If your affiliate model doesn't already include an embedded staff member at your primary school(s) served, you may want to consider making this transition before attempting a Collective Impact initiative.

♦ Develop a Work Plan for Each Opportunity

For each opportunity, identify:

1. Lead person
2. Activities
3. Resources and support
4. Timing and deadlines
5. Measures of success

Attachment C provides a template to record this information, and Attachment D provides a sample work plan.

Step 3: Execute and Refine Plan

Now that you have a plan, it is time to put that plan into action. The Collective Impact Coordinator and backbone agency will play critical roles in ensuring that the project stays on track. Because you have included common metrics into your design, the team will be able to regularly assess progress and make midstream corrections. Don't forget to celebrate successes along the way!

Execute and Refine the Action Plan

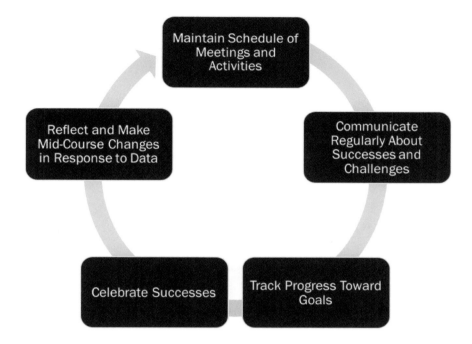

As the figure demonstrates, the implementation of the action plan must be consistently monitored with ongoing communication throughout the process. In addition, it is important to use the defined metrics in order to understand what is working and what might need to be changed. Meetings should include time for reflection, and the team should support evolution and change, as flexibility and openness will be core success factors.

From the Front Lines

When the pilot team implemented their action plan, the process ran relatively smoothly because they put so much effort into aligning expectations and outlining responsibilities from the outset. However, at times in the process it was clear that—despite the common goals established—organizations had slightly differing agendas. In fact, all the partner organizations found it necessary to compromise at one time or another. Team members found that the Collective Impact Coordinator's ability to set a collaborative and respectful tone and ensure that all "voices" were heard in the progress meetings was essential to the progress made. In turn, it was crucial for all partners to enter the process believing that each member organization had something valuable to contribute as well as important lessons to learn from others.

ATTACHMENT A

Interview Guide

Use these questions as a guide, not a script, when speaking with partners about their experience in the schools and working with students.

Introduction: Take Stock in Children is interested in spearheading a Collective Impact project. This is based on research that says that when partners align their goals and actions, greater impact on children and families can result. The first step in this work is understanding the existing landscape.

Goals

1) What is your organization's mission?

2) How do you measure your success? How do you know when you've reached your goals?

3) What helps make you successful?

4) Which students do you aim to serve?

5) Who decides/decided your goals?

History

1) What is your history in this school?

2) When did your program start working here?

3) How did the organization decide to start working here?

4) Has any work around Collective Impact ever been tried before? How did it go?

Organizational Structure

1) Who are the staff based in this school?

2) What other resources are available to you in this school from your organization?

Partnerships

1) Who are your partners?

2) How do you work together?

3) Are there other systems that you are aligned with (e.g., school improvement plan)?

4) What other initiatives are you aware of (either internal to the school or external partners) that might be aligned with your goals?

5) Who else should be part of this discussion?

Program

1) How does your program work?

2) What are your main activities?

3) What is your calendar?

Challenges

1) What are the main challenges you face?

2) What do you do to counteract these challenges?

Overall Landscape

1) What student needs do you think are met by the school and its partners?

2) What needs are unmet? What gaps are there?

3) What do you think is working well here? What could be better?

ATTACHMENT B

Collective Impact Partners

PARTNER NAME	PROGRAM SERVICES	GOALS	STRENGTHS	BARRIERS

ATTACHMENT C

Action Planning Template

OBJECTIVE
LEAD PERSON
ACTIVITIES
RESOURCES AND SUPPORT
TIMING AND DEADLINES
MEASURES OF SUCCESS

ATTACHMENT D

Action Planning Template Sample

OBJECTIVE: Develop a common language with partners at the table to ensure that efforts are not being duplicated and that information is being shared efficiently
Lead Person: Collective Impact Coordinator
Activities: • Identify the students who are being served by multiple providers. • Collect and share data about common students to determine where services are overlapping and where gaps exist. • Develop efficiencies to make information sharing easier, such as streamlining referral forms. • Determine the points where services from one partner end and others begin to ensure continuous impact and aligned efforts. • Utilize leadership meetings with partners present to facilitate the data sharing and alignment process.
Resources and Support: Principal Leadership from partnership organizations
Timing and Deadlines: Planning meetings will take place on a regular basis throughout the year, the frequency of which will be determined in January during the Collective Impact Plan partner feedback meeting.
Measures of Success: Improved student academic indicators, such as attendance and grades as well as a decrease in behavioral referrals, will indicate success. Also, a more efficient information-sharing process across partners will offer a more complete picture of student progress over time and better indicate where additional support is needed if students are moving off track.

Civitas Strategies, Andrew Jackson Collective Impact Plan, 2015.

ATTACHMENT E

References

Civitas Strategies. (October 2015). *Take Stock in Children: The Collective Impact Approach, Confidential.* Melrose, MA.

Civitas Strategies. (December 2017). *Directors Certification Series Session #1.* Lynnfield, MA.

FSG and SSIR. (January 19, 2011). *Collective Impact: Creating Large-Scale Social Change.* Retrieved from https://www.fsg.org/sites/default/files/tools-and-resources/Collective_Impact_Webinar_presentation.pdf

Kania, J. and Kramer, M. (2011). Collective Impact. *Stanford Social Innovation Review. 9* (1). Retrieved from https://ssir.org/articles/entry/collective_impact.

National Governors Association, Talent Pipeline Policy Academy. (2014). *Collective Impact: Leading Change to Achieve Results.* Retrieved from https://www.nga.org/files/live/sites/NGA/files/pdf/2014/1410NGATPAPolicyAcademyCollectiveImpactPresentation.pdf.

Strive Together. *Impact.* Retrieved from https://www.strivetogether.org/impact/.

Take Stock in Children. (2015). *2015-2016 Collective Impact Plan, Andrew Jackson High School.*

Take Stock
Innovation Collection:
Financial Aid & Alternative
Scholarship Models

Take Stock in
Children®

The contents of this manual were developed under a grant from the
U.S. Department of Education, Investing in Innovation (i3) Program.
However, those contents do not necessarily represent the policy of
the U.S. Department of Education, and you should not assume
endorsement by the federal government.

Table of Contents

ACKNOWLEDGEMENTS

Take Stock in Children (TSIC) would like to thank and acknowledge the UNISON team, who has worked tirelessly to launch and successfully implement the innovations supported by TSIC's Investing in Innovation (i3) grant. This team, led by Judy Saylor, Director of Program Growth and Innovation, includes Tiara Arline, Sara Buckley, Tiffany Givens, Amy Grunder, Roxanne Jordan, and Luz Rodriguez. The i3 grant program is ultimately about helping grantees reach scale. Through the hard work of this team, the UNISON project innovations will impact over 8,500 students per year through 45 independent affiliates across the TSIC network.

Finally, TSIC would also like to recognize Gary Romano and the Civitas Strategies team for guiding the codification and scaling process of the innovations that the i3 UNISON project is developing.

The increased number of students served and the continually growing demand for our local programs mean that UNISON innovations will provide the network with opportunities that efficiently use resources and maintain a high level of programmatic quality and service delivery. Scaling these elements will not only benefit the TSIC network, but also accelerate the progress of national scaling efforts. Network-wide adoption will effectively result in additional proof points and data, contributing to a climate conducive to national uptake.

Introduction

For over 24 years, Take Stock in Children (TSIC) has offered students a way out of poverty and into higher education through scholarships, mentors, and hope. The organization was founded in 1995 by a group of education, community, and business leaders frustrated by the large number of at-risk children in Florida not graduating from high school, not accessing higher education, and as a result, being shut out of life-changing jobs and opportunities. Together, they created a simple, yet transformative solution. Students are recruited in middle and high school and receive comprehensive support, primarily during high school and through post-secondary graduation. Each student benefits from weekly meetings with a volunteer adult mentor as well as professional post-secondary college and career coaching services. Students also sign a contract, agreeing to remain drug- and crime-free, maintain good attendance and grades, meet regularly with their mentor, and attend college readiness workshops. In exchange, students receive a post-secondary scholarship to mitigate financial barriers to higher education.

The results for students in poverty have been extraordinary:

96% of Take Stock in Children students graduate high school on time

92% of Take Stock in Children students enter post-secondary education

68% of The Stock in Children Students complete post-secondary education, compared to the state average of 27% for at-risk students in poverty

A recent study conducted by TSIC found that there are 145,000 students throughout the state of Florida who could benefit from TSIC's model. The overall success of the program, as demonstrated by the results, is encouraging affiliates to find innovative solutions to increase the number of students served across the state.

The financial barrier to college is one of the greatest challenges that at-risk students and their families face when it comes to post-secondary access and completion. Throughout its history, TSIC has made great strides to mitigate this barrier through the purchase of Florida Prepaid Scholarships. A key feature of the TSIC model is to provide a Florida Prepaid Scholarship to each student enrolled in the program. Though this proves a powerful incentive and post-secondary success strategy, providing scholarships to every TSIC student is also unsustainable as a singular solution due to the costs of the initial investment required to purchase the scholarships and the ongoing management of the scholarship awards.

The Florida Prepaid Scholarship will remain a central feature of the Take Stock in Children model. However, UNISON, Upward Bound, and other projects within the TSIC network have identified the opportunity to serve a greater number of students via alternative strategies, such as intensive financial aid counseling and support. Ideas like "last dollar in" scholarships have also proved an impactful solution.

Additionally, affiliates have experienced success with helping students access early college and other programs that offer college credit in high school. By taking advantage of these opportunities, students can reduce the cost of post-secondary education, as well as build the confidence needed to complete college-level courses. The TSIC network is interested in forging credit-bearing pathways for students beginning in high school so they can stay on track throughout post-secondary experiences and ultimately complete their degree.

This financial aid and scholarship manual is the result of the codification of best and promising practices and strategies utilized throughout the TSIC network and beyond. The purpose of this manual is to guide programs as they establish and launch alternative scholarship models. Material covered in this manual includes:

- Strategies for reducing the cost of college.
- Best practices for securing financial aid and tools of implementation.
- Examples of alternative and "last dollar in" scholarships.
- Tools for establishing and managing alternative scholarships.

Implementing new strategies and tools can be challenging. If you have any questions not covered in the manual or feedback in general you would like to share, please contact the TSIC State Office or your Regional Director.

This manual is intended to offer TSIC affiliate program leadership with information about the financial resources available to their students to help them access and complete college. The second section of this manual covers how programs, whether run through an education foundation or not, can consider the strategic viability of creating new scholarship opportunities for students. Program leadership may decide to disseminate this information to staff, who may in turn incorporate it into their programs.

CHAPTER 1 — Strategies to Break the Financial Barrier

The Cost of College

The average annual cost of a four-year college education in the state of Florida for students living off campus is approximately $20,000 (IPEDS, US Department of Education). Of those expenses, roughly 72% are non-tuition related; these costs include books, supplies, and living expenses. Several strategies can help students reduce these costs, increasing their likelihood of college completion.

Chapter 1 will provide an overview of strategies to help make college more affordable for students. While the Florida Prepaid Scholarship will remain a central feature of the Take Stock in Children model, the purpose of this chapter is to offer several approaches to helping students access additional existing resources that may help make college more affordable. Part 1 will discuss ways to reduce costs of college through dual-enrollment programs, and Part 2 will discuss financial aid resources.

PART 1: REDUCING THE COST OF COLLEGE

One of the most effective strategies for reducing the cost of college is via enrollment in early college, dual credit programs, or other programs that offer college credit in high school. Part 1 of this chapter will discuss how dual enrollment works and then offer some resources for helping students access dual enrollment opportunities.

Dual Enrollment/Early College FAQs:

- ✓ What is dual enrollment? It includes accelerated courses in high school that allow students to simultaneously earn credit toward both high school completion and a career certificate or an associate's or bachelor's degree at a Florida public higher education institute.

- ✓ Who qualifies? Students in grades 9-12 with an unweighted GPA of 3.0 may enroll in college credit courses. Students in grades 9-12 with an unweighted GPA of 2.0 may enroll in career certificate courses. Students must maintain the required GPA to retain dual enrollment eligibility. Students must also achieve a minimum score on a common placement test.

- ✓ Where do students take classes? Typically, students attend regularly scheduled classes on a local college campus. Instructors typically do not know students are in the dual enrollment program unless the student offers that information.

Dual Enrollment Benefits

Studies have shown that students who participate in dual enrollment programs are more successful academically. For example, a 2006 Florida study found that students who had participated in the state university system's dual enrollment program had higher

SAT scores and higher GPAs than their counterparts who had not participated.

In addition, there are a number of financial benefits to dual enrollment. These are as follows:

- College tuition and fees are waived for students in dual enrollment courses.
- Textbooks are loaned free of charge to students in public high school, resulting in significant savings.
- Students receive both college credit and credit toward high school graduation requirements.

Students must apply for dual enrollment courses through their guidance department and be approved to do so.

Dual Enrollment Challenges

A significant challenge facing students who pursue dual enrollment programs is transportation. It poses a major barrier for many students, given that most high schools do not offer dual enrollment opportunities on campus; most parents are not available to transport their children to and from a college campus mid-day; and public transportation is not always available.

Some models address this issue. One is a full immersion model, where students spend their full day at the community college. Another is to have a cohort of students enroll in one community college, and then have the college provide busing for them mid-day. Finally, students can research opportunities to receive stipends from Uber or similar platforms.

Another challenge affiliate staff have noted is ensuring students have the academic and social maturity

to handle college-level coursework while still in high school. Several interviewees noted that they have observed students attempt dual enrollment and then fail the coursework, a disheartening experience that often leads students to drop out of higher education endeavors entirely. It also means students receive an "F" on their college transcript, which could impact their future chances of college admission. Therefore, it is crucial that the student is fully prepared for the challenge and that a system of supports and interventions are in place in case the student struggles with the academic, social, or logistical expectations.

For some students, earning Advanced Placement credits at their high school may be preferable (and if so, it is always important to ensure that the higher education programs the student is seeking will accept the credits).

See Attachment A for a sample worksheet to use when comparing the costs of college enrollment vs. dual enrollment.

Other Practices for Reducing the Cost of College

1. As an organization, you can work to develop reciprocal partnerships with local post-secondary institutions in the community, particularly if the majority of your program's students tend to choose a particular campus. Many affiliates have exchanged campus recruitment efforts for benefits for their students who choose to attend, such as additional academic supports or discounts on books and other materials. Some campuses have even created TSIC-student specific scholarships.

2. Create a comparison chart to educate parents and students on the cost difference in course credits between various local institutions; also, counsel

students on how this may impact the overall cost of their education. For example, most degree programs will require students to take English 101 during their freshman year. However, the cost of this class may vary greatly from campus to campus. Students interested in more expensive institutions may benefit from taking introductory courses at a lower-cost campus and then transferring the credits to their desired program.

3. Ensure students are aware of the community resources available to help subsidize cost of living while they are in school, particularly if a financial emergency should occur. It may be worthwhile to consider partnering with local organizations as well: for example, food banks that could provide sustenance to students in need or locally-owned shops that might be willing to give students a discount on textbooks, school supplies, etc. For housing, cooperative or subsidized housing may be available to students at a reduced rate, both on and off campus.

4. Begin counseling students early on (for example, in 9th grade) as to the costs of attending post-secondary programming, including cost of living. Ensure students and parents are fully aware that the TSIC Florida Prepaid Scholarship will not cover all costs and that they should begin planning early to mitigate this challenge, with support and resources offered by affiliate staff. Ensure students and parents understand how good grades and high SAT/ACT scores can impact the number of scholarship and financial aid opportunities available.

See Attachment B for a worksheet that can be used to help students and their families compare the costs of different college option.

EXERCISE 1: Review Dual Enrollment Options with Your Students

Many students are not aware of the opportunities and benefits related to dual enrollment. Be sure to cover the following with them:

1) Explain what dual enrollment means. Underscore the fact that it means taking college-level courses while still in high school and that the courses may be more rigorous than what they have experienced in the past.

2) Review their eligibility. Check that the student's GPA is 3.0 or greater if pursuing a college-level course, or 2.0 or greater if pursuing a career certificate course.

3) Review the courses. The Florida Department of Education keeps an updated list of eligible courses on its Dual Enrollment website: http://www.fldoe.org/schools/higher-ed/fl-college-system/academic-student-affairs/dual-enrollment.stml

4) Consider transportation issues. As stated in the previous section, lack of transportation can be a major barrier for students. Look into whether the college has any transportation options or if the students' school district provides busing for student cohorts participating in the same dual enrollment program.

PART 2: INCREASING ACCESS TO FINANCIAL AID

Another important strategy for reducing the costs of college is accessing financial aid resources. The information below will help your program support students in applying for financial aid.

Definition

Financial aid is typically any grant, scholarship, or loan available to help students cover expenses related to college. This aid can be provided through federal and state agencies, colleges, foundations, and corporations. The amount of financial aid a student receives is determined by a number of factors, including state, federal, or institutional guidelines, as well as the cost of tuition and living expenses. Grants and scholarships do not need to be repaid while loans must be repaid at a later date, with payments typically commencing upon graduation or withdrawal from college. Interest rates and repayment terms vary by loan program and should be read carefully before accepting.

Importance of FAFSA

The Free Application for Federal Student Aid (FAFSA) is a form that current and prospective college students should submit annually. Information provided on the FAFSA form is the primary source of data that determines eligibility for financial aid from federal, state, and institutional programs. The FAFSA is not typically required for private grants and scholarships, though need-based grants and scholarships may request similar information.

Pell Grants

The Federal Pell Grant Program provides need-based grants to low-income undergraduate students.

✓ Unlike a loan, a Pell Grant does not have to be repaid.

✓ The maximum Pell Grant for the 2016-2017 school year was approximately $6000.

✓ The amount awarded depends on financial need, cost to attend school, status as a full-time or part-time student, and plans to attend for a full academic year or less.

✓ To apply, students must submit a completed FAFSA form.

Pell Grant funds are limited each year; early applicants are more likely to receive the total amount they qualify for. Go to https://studentaid.ed.gov/sa/types/grants-scholarships/pell for current Pell Grant information.

FAFSA Completion

Each year approximately 50% of Florida high school seniors do not complete the FAFSA. As a result, Florida College Access Now (FCAN) estimates that Florida high school graduates leave behind over $100 million in Pell Grants each year because they did not complete the FAFSA form.

In addition to its role in securing aid, FAFSA completion is also a leading indicator of college enrollment. Students who have been accepted to college but do not complete a FAFSA form are less likely to enroll than their peers who do complete the form.

Increasing FAFSA Completion Rate

Given that too many students are not taking advantage of financial aid opportunities, it proves crucial that Take Stock in Children affiliates educate students and families about the FAFSA and provide ongoing resources and reminders to support students in completing their FAFSA forms.

Keep in mind these important facts about FAFSA completion:

- Students have higher levels of FAFSA completion when adults provide support, structure, and resources from the beginning of the application to final submission.
- Take Stock in Children's recent Upward Bound program in Miami-Dade County provided individual advising to students in filling out forms and walking them through the entire application process; this initiative saw a 98% FAFSA completion rate and 92% postsecondary enrollment rate as of March 2017.
- Students who file their FAFSA in October, November, or December receive more than twice the funding from federal, state, and college sources as students who file later in the year.

To increase FAFSA completion rates, some affiliates have partnered with local college campuses to hold "FAFSA Completion" events with accepted students. This is a great way to ensure that forms are completed in a timely manner and helps begin to build working relationships between students and campus staff. Other affiliates noted the importance of engaging translators for all FAFSA workshops involving students' families, helping to ensure that parents and guardians have a full understanding of the application process.

Other Practices in Securing Financial Aid

The following are some additional best practices in working with students to secure financial aid:

Common Understanding	Processes & Deadlines	Be Proactive	Consistent Reminders
• Ensure that parents, guardians, and students have a common understanding of the financial aid process, deadlines, and requirements. When meeting with students to discuss financial aid options, invite parents and guardians to attend as well.	• Ensure that students understand processes and deadlines for renewing or continuing financial aid each year, as well as any academic or credit/course load requirements.	• Include financial aid as a routine part of the college search process for every student, rather than as an add-on or afterthought. Educate students regarding ongoing fiscal responsibility throughout their post-secondary career. For example, some students may have funds left over from various grants at the end of a term and may benefit from advisement on how funds could best be used productively.	• Set up a system via text or email to remind both students and their parents and guardians as the deadlines for the FAFSA and other financial aid approach.

For more information about financial aid, please visit http://www.floridastudentfinancialaid.org

Exercise 2: Create a FAFSA Completion Campaign

Step 1: Set a goal

Start the process by setting a goal for FAFSA completion and create a simple Excel spreadsheet to track completion numbers.

Step 2: Host FAFSA completion events

Schedule several events for students and their families. These can include informational events to educate students and families about the FAFSA, why it's important and what it entails, as well as events where families can work on the FAFSA with available staff support.

Step 3: Remind, remind, remind! Use texting and social media to remind students of deadlines and encourage them to complete their FAFSA as early as possible.

For a comprehensive set of resources to support students in FAFSA completion, visit the FAFSA Challenge website of the Florida College Access Network at: http://floridacollegeaccess.org/initiatives/florida-fafsa-challenge/

PART 3: USING ALTERNATIVE SCHOLARSHIP

Unlike some types of financial aid, scholarships are typically merit-based and do not require the funds to be repaid. While this makes scholarships highly desirable, it also means they can be extremely competitive and are typically not tailored to meet the needs of historically underserved populations. In addition, many scholarships are only one-year in length, making them an unreliable financial aid source.

This section will help programs understand alternative scholarships and support their students in applying for these opportunities.

Types of Scholarships

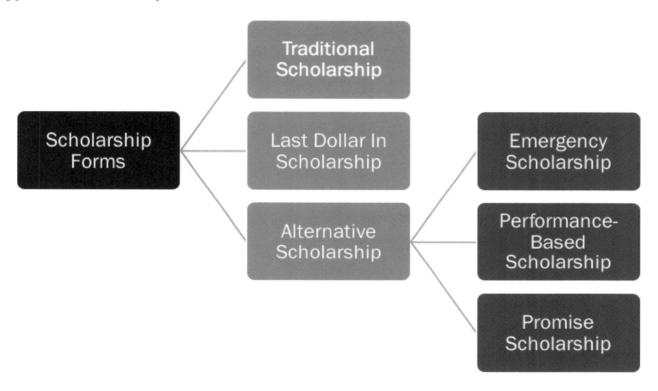

Traditional Scholarships: These awards are given to students to help pay for college tuition, and students do not need to be repay them.

Last Dollar In: These scholarships are intended to fill the gap between students' financial aid and the costs of college, such as computers, books and supplies, room and board, and even graduation expenses.

"Last Dollar In" scholarships are awarded to students whose official Expected Family Contribution (EFC), located on their Student Aid Report, and financial aid package totals are less than the cost of tuition and fees. "Last Dollar In" scholarships vary greatly state to state.

Source:https://www.scholarships.com/financial-aid/college-scholarships/scholarships-by-type/last-dollar-scholarship/

Alternative Scholarships: These resemble traditional scholarships in that they are gifted or "free" money that does not require repayment. However, alternative scholarships differ from their traditional counterparts in important ways. Primarily, alternative scholarships seek to meet needs unmet by other financial aid and scholarships. Alternative scholarships are designed to serve any community and meet any existing need.

Each of the following scholarship types are examples of alternative scholarships.

- **Emergency Scholarships:** These alternative scholarships offer financial assistance for students facing unexpected hardship. The hardship must threaten the student's ability to persist in or complete college. The scholarships are typically offered one time and total less than $1,500.

- **Performance-Based Scholarships:** These alternative scholarships are financial aid for low-income students, contingent upon completion of certain academic benchmarks. They are paid directly to students in multiple disbursements throughout the term and are intended to supplement other financial aid (federal and state).

- **Promise Scholarships:** These alternative scholarships are institutional or place-based initiatives that offer funding for students who live in the program's geographic area. Some Promise Scholarships require completion of college prep programs, minimum GPA, specific attendance benchmarks, and/or completion of career plan.

Best Practices for Encouraging the Use of Alternative Scholarships

- Ensure that parents, guardians, and students have a common understanding of and access to resources for finding alternative scholarships. When meeting with students to discuss alternative scholarships, invite parents and guardians to attend as well.

- Consider offering incentives for scholarship application completion; for example, one affiliate hosted a "Cash for College" initiative, offering students $10 for each scholarship application completed and submitted.

- Assign staff to compile a list of additional scholarship opportunities students may be eligible for. High school guidance counselors are an excellent resource for this. Ensure the scholarship list is regularly updated for student and staff use and disseminated to both students and parents. Some examples are shown on the next page.

Examples of Additional Scholarship Opportunities

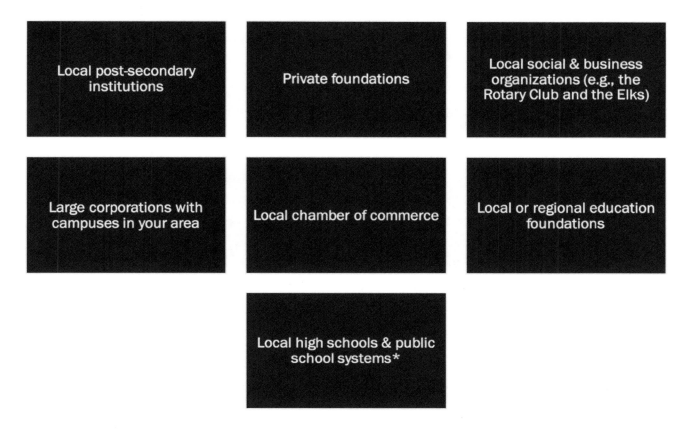

*For example, Pinellas County Foundation offers a range of scholarship opportunities to students graduating from the Pinellas County Schools.

Alternative Scholarship Resources

See below for a list of additional resources on alternative scholarship options in the state of Florida:

- Florida DOE – www.floridastudentfinancialaid.org
- Southern Scholarship Foundation – https://www.southernscholarship.org/
- University of Florida – https://admissions.ufl.edu/afford/scholarships
- Florida State University – https://education.fsu.edu/student-resources/scholarships-and-aid
- University of Central Florida – https://finaid.ucf.edu/types-of-aid/
- Gulf Coast State College Foundation – https://www.gulfcoast.edu/foundation/
- TRIO – https://fltrio.weebly.com/scholarship.html

See Attachment C for Financial Aid FAQs to Use with Families.

Exercise 3: Help Students Identify Alternative Scholarships

Step 1: Evaluate eligibility

Many scholarships are merit-based, so start by working with students to identify which common criteria they meet. What is their GPA? Have they completed college prep courses?

Step 2: Search!

Several scholarship search engines are available to help students find scholarships that are a good fit for them. Some search engines include Scholly, College Board's Scholarship Search, FastWeb, and Scholarships. com.

Work with students to find all of the scholarships they can apply for. Go for quantity—the more applications submitted, the better their chances of success. Work with them to develop a scholarship calendar that includes the deadlines for all the scholarships for which they should apply.

Step 3: Help students tell their story

When writing essays for scholarships, be sure to help students find the stories they can share that demonstrate what makes them special. Students should save all of their essays in order to re-use parts for other applications. Finally, students should be sure to have a presentable presence on social media. Their online presence is a part of their story.

CHAPTER 2 — Establishing an Alternative Scholarship

The previous chapter discussed ways that Take Stock in Children affiliates can leverage existing resources and opportunities to support students in reducing college costs. In addition, Take Stock in Children may choose to establish an alternative scholarship in order to provide increased financial opportunities to students pursuing a higher education degree.

This section is intended to help TSIC affiliates consider whether to develop additional non-traditional scholarships that can help students complete college.

These scholarships may be small amounts of money that can make significant impact on a student's ability to access college. For example, life events such as a car breaking down, an illness of a parent or child, or a crashed computer could threaten a student's ability to participate in college. Non-traditional scholarships that can cover emergency costs could provide a huge benefit.

PART 1: OVERVIEW OF ESTABLISHING A SCHOLARSHIP

Some critical questions to consider before establishing an alternative scholarship include the following:

- What is the problem you want to solve?
- What community are you hoping to serve?
- How will you measure if you are making an impact?

Answering some of these questions may be relatively easy. For example, you may know that your priority is to serve all Take Stock in Children students in your region. However, a deeper dive into the available data may suggest that a specific sub-population of students has a higher need or has had access to fewer scholarships. Utilizing any data available or seeking out additional information through students will ensure scholarships are designed to meet specific needs.

Using a "Last Dollar In" Model

In TSIC's current model, each student receives a Florida Prepaid Scholarship. Typically, when the student attends an institution of higher education, the Florida Prepaid Scholarship is expended first— ahead of some federal, state, or institutional financial aid. With a "last dollar in" scholarship, the student first taps all their financial aid—public and private—and scholarship funding is applied only to the difference between the financial aid award and the funds needed to attend college. In many cases, students require little (under $1,000) or no funding annually. By encouraging students to utilize all of the available public and private aid before scholarship funding, the amount of scholarship funding required is much smaller and can be more easily generated through campaigns and donations. Using a "last dollar in" model does require that students, TSIC staff, and colleges work together to leverage other financial resources.

Effective Scholarship Models

While scholarships may differ in duration, amount, and requirements, some key practices contribute to efficient and effective scholarship use. Scholarship models are most effective when they:

- Are Renewable – Uncertainty of funding is one of the major barriers to college completion. When students know funds are renewable from year to year (if they meet the requirements), it can help mitigate anxiety about funding.

- Are Predictable – The more uncertainty around a scholarship, the less likely students are to utilize it. Scholarships should be predictable in terms of timelines, requirements, and availability of funding.

- Are Simple and Transparent – Are the eligibility requirements, timelines, application process, and availability of funds easy to understand and complete?

- Supplement Institutional Funds – Scholarships providing gap funding (the difference between available aid and necessary costs) are some of the most effective in supporting college completion.

- Incorporate Incentives for Academic Success – Incentives not only encourage academic success but also reinforce the association between hard work and effort with compensation, a critical concept for career building and persistence.

- Include Non-financial Support Services – These services include mentoring, academic and career counseling, academic tutoring, and internship placement.

Emergency Scholarships

Emergency scholarships—one-time small grants given to students to cover unexpected life circumstances—can be both highly effective for aiding students in the completion of a degree and logistically challenging for affiliate staff to facilitate. Affiliate staff interviewed in this manual's development noted situations where students have had to drop out of post-secondary programming because they could not afford a car repair or monthly rent payment; in these types of situations, the granting of a relatively small amount of money might make all the difference in students' ability to continue their studies. However, when developing an emergency scholarship program, it proves crucial to clearly outline the parameters of the grant and ensure that all stakeholders are in agreement as to how grants will be administered; this mitigates the challenge of affiliate staff subjectively determining what constitutes an "emergency" and which students are eligible to receive funding.

PART 2: STEPS TO ESTABLISHING A SCHOLARSHIP

The figure below provides an overview of the steps to establish a scholarship. The following sections will provide more details and guidelines for each step.

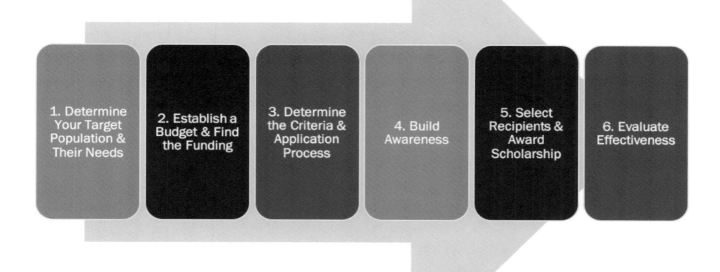

Step 1: Determine Your Target Population & Their Needs

In order to leverage limited resources, identifying the specific sub-population of students eligible for the scholarship proves important. You can access existing data as well as engage in interviews to gather the necessary information to make this decision.

Exercise 4: Who should receive the scholarship, and for what?

Step 1: Analyze the data

This first step involves reviewing and analyzing any available data on college completion in the community. One key place to find this data is on the Florida Department of Education's data website: www.flodoe.org/schools/higher-ed/fl-college-system/data-reports/transeparency-accountability.stml. Following are key data to consider:

- College completion trends for students—specifically, what percentage of students in the community have completed college within 6 years?
- Trends in completion barriers for students—what main reasons do students in the community cite for not completing college?
- Demographic information specifically related to completion.

Step 2: Review existing scholarships

Find information about available, existing scholarships. Strive to not duplicate efforts. For example, if most scholarships are only available to students pursuing a four-year degree, you may consider establishing a scholarship for students pursuing a degree at a two-year college. Create an Excel sheet that lists the scholarships for which students in the community are eligible, and then look for the gaps.

Step 3: Interview stakeholders

In addition to reviewing the above information, you may want to interview key stakeholders to help paint a fuller picture of students' challenges when facing financial barriers to college access and completion. Interview school guidance counselors and other administrators, financial aid staff in local colleges, and students themselves. Key questions to ask include the following:

- Which financial resources are you/your students taking advantage of?
- As you prepare yourself/your students for college, what are your/their major financial concerns?
- For college administrators: What specific financial concerns tend to come up for students on financial aid at your institution?

After engaging in this full analysis, you should be able to identify a target population for the scholarship as well as a specific purpose for the funds.

Step 2: Establish a Budget & Find the Funding

Based on your research and capacity, determine an ideal amount of funding to raise. This amount will depend on the following key questions:

- How many students do you hope to serve each year?
- How much will the scholarship grant be?
- What is your internal fundraising capacity?
- Do you have existing or prospective donors lined up who will be interested in this opportunity?
- What will be the annual costs of administering and promoting the scholarship?

If your goal is to fund an emergency scholarship of $1,500 to 20 students each year ($30,000), along with any expenses to manage the scholarship (approximately $10,000), you may determine that raising $40,000 annually may not be feasible. Instead, set a goal of two or three times the annual operating amount. This will provide the initial investment you need, allowing you to then continue fundraising and investing funds to create a sustainable scholarship program. You should plan to consult a tax professional to understand any legal or fiscal obligations.

When deciding which funders to approach, consider how their priorities align with the target population and the need impacted by the scholarship. Utilize both data and human experiences to paint a compelling picture of how their gift and contribution will impact and sustain success. As mentioned, finding donors willing to help establish the first two or three years of the scholarship can be especially effective—and then regularly providing updates on college completion outcomes and scholarship effectiveness proves crucial as well.

Establishing a Timeline

The ASRT Education and Research Foundation suggests mapping out a timeline for internal use by the scholarship administration team. This timeline should include all activities, as exemplified below.

Activity	Begin Date	Deadline
Program development	Summer	Late fall
Fundraising	Summer and fall	Spring
Advertising	January	April 15
Application period	January–March	April 15
Award announcement	May 1	May 8

Exercise 5: Create a budget and fundraising goal

A. Individual scholarship award amount: _____

B. Number of scholarships awarded per year:

_____

C. A x B = _____

D. Multiply C x 3 years of initial funding:_____

E. Add at least $10,000 to D, accounting for costs to manage the grants:

_____

Now list the potential donors who would be motivated to help establish a new scholarship for your students, plus the amount of funding you could realistically raise from these funders. The total of all these should equal the number on line E.

Funder: _____ Amount: _____

Funder:_____ Amount: _____

Funder: _____ Amount: _____

Funder: _____ Amount: _____

Funder: _____ Amount: _____

Funder: _____ Amount: _____

Step 3: Determine the Criteria & Application Process

Establish the criteria – Aim to have a clear and accessible application process. This starts with establishing the criteria for the scholarship. You can utilize your data to help determine eligibility criteria. For example, if you are providing emergency scholarships, information from current and former students about the types of emergencies that threatened completion may be useful. Your criteria should be easy to interpret and broad enough to capture the target population and need, but not so broad that a high number of non-target students apply. Forming a small workgroup of stakeholders to help shape the criteria may be helpful.

Create the application -- When creating the application itself, be sure to develop an online application. Online forms are more accessible and will expedite the review process. Several websites will generate an application or form using a template, such as Jotform.com and Zoho.com. Keep in mind that long applications may discourage students from applying, so keep it to one to two pages and only collect necessary information.

Set the deadline – Most scholarships have deadlines in the spring (January through May). However, depending on the type of scholarship, you may have additional deadlines through the rest of the year, or in the case of an emergency scholarship, you may have a rolling deadline so students can apply as the need arises. A good practice is a minimum 60-day application window, with another two to three weeks to select recipients and communicate award notices.

The following are some common components of scholarship applications:

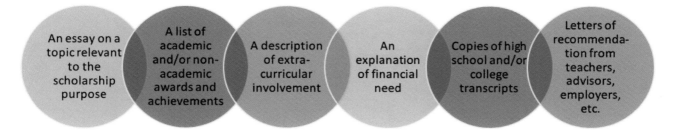

Step 4: Build Awareness

Marketing and awareness-building can occur year-round and may be especially intensive in the weeks leading up to and during the application window. Strategies for marketing will depend on the target population and the availability of funds. Following are some suggested marketing strategies:

- Webinars for school guidance counselors and/or partner organizations that work on college access
- Printed one-page flyers/brochures
- In-person information sessions for students
- Google and/or Facebook advertisements

Step 5: Select Recipients & Award Scholarship

Select recipients – To ensure a fair process, it is good practice to establish a review committee that consists of at least four people, with a ratio of one staff member to three community stakeholders. These may be current or former students, scholarship staff, and a community member or other stakeholder. Create an evaluation rubric for applications so that review committee members can score applicants against a common set of criteria. Create a survey form or Excel spreadsheet to capture committee members' scores. Then you can consolidate the scores and generate a list of students who are the strongest fit for the scholarship. Finally, gather the committee to discuss the applicants and pare down the list to the students who will be selected.

Award the scholarship – Recipients should be notified via mail, email, and/or phone. It is important to collect information for more than one method of contact so recipients can be reached. Be sure to indicate how the funds may and may not be used, when students can expect disbursement of funds, a reminder of any ongoing eligibility requirements (credit/course load, GPA, etc.), information on renewal deadlines, and who to contact with questions or concerns.

Step 6: Evaluate Effectiveness

The appropriate level of evaluation will depend upon the type of scholarship. In the case of promise or performance-based scholarship models that are renewable, a longitudinal evaluation that tracks student completion rates and academic achievements may be useful to demonstrate impact. For any scholarship, at a minimum you will want to be able to demonstrate that the funds have reached the target population and need, how many students were awarded funds, the total amount given, and the range or average amount of individual scholarships. This data is critical for taxes and legal purposes and will also help you in continuing to advocate for investments from funders.

ATTACHMENT A

Compare the Costs:
College Enrollment vs. Dual Enrollment

This worksheet helps students understand the costs of college vs. the costs of dual enrollment courses.

Item	College Enrollment Cost Per Semester	Dual Enrollment Cost
Tuition and fees	$3000	Waived
Books and supplies	$600	Waived
Room and board	$5200	
Transportation	$800	
Other expenses (typically including student health insurance, cell phone, laundry, and other personal costs)	$1400	
Total	$11,000	

Source: http://www.flbog.edu/board/office/budget/tuition.php

ATTACHMENT B

Comparing College Costs Worksheet

1	Calculations for College, One Year	College A	College B	College C	College D	College E
	First Year Educational Costs					
	Tuition					
	Fees					
	Books/Supplies					
	Transportation					
	Room & Board					
	Miscellaneous					
1A	**Total Cost of Attendance**					
2	**Financial Aid Components**					
2A	**Gift Aid**					
	Institutional Scholarship #1					
	Institutional Scholarship #2					
	Institutional Grant					
	Federal Pell Grant					
	Other Grant (SEOG, etc.)					
2A	**Sub-Total Gift Aid**					

2B	Self-Help					
	Federal Subsidized Stafford Loan					
	Federal Unsubsidized Stafford Loan					
	Perkins Loan					
	Institutional Loan/ Financing					
	PLUS Loan					
	Federal Work Study					
2B	Sub-Total Self-Help					
3	Total Financial Aid (2A+2B)					
4	Remaining Out-of-Pocket Expense (1A - 2A - 2B)					
5	Total Expense to Family (1A - 2A)					

*See next page for further explanation of these categories.

1A – When comparing college costs, begin by making sure you are including the total cost of attendance for each institution. Schools will frequently list just their tuition or include tuition plus room and board. This can be misleading as you will encounter additional expenses that could total as much as an additional $10,000, depending on factors such as where you live and your intended program of study. Keep in mind that out-of-state costs are greater at state universities.

2A – Gift aid represents support you receive for which there is no expected payback. Sources of this aid are the institution, the government, and local organizations. Scholarships are merit-based, and renewal is often contingent on the satisfaction of specified academic or performance criteria. Grants are based on your demonstrated need as determined by the FAFSA or CSS Profile. The selection of gift aid is optional.

2B – Self-help includes funding sources you can draw upon to cover college costs for which you are accountable. The Federal Subsidized Stafford Loan, the Perkins Loan, and Federal Work-Study are need-based (FAFSA). The other financing is accessible regardless of need. The selection of self-help funding is optional.

3 – Total financial aid, gift aid, and self-help, available from all sources.

4 – The remaining "out-of-pocket" expense includes the costs of attendance that may not be covered by any form of financial aid in the financial aid award letter.

5 – Total expense to family includes "self-help" financial aid and remaining "out-of-pocket" expense.

ATTACHMENT C

Financial Aid and Scholarship FAQs for Families

What Does College Cost?

- Average cost of four-year college in the state of Florida for a student living off campus is approximately $20,000 (*IPEDS, US Department of Education).
- Approximately 72% of costs are non-tuition related. These non-tuition related expenses could include books, supplies, and living expenses.

What Can Be Done to Reduce the Cost of College?

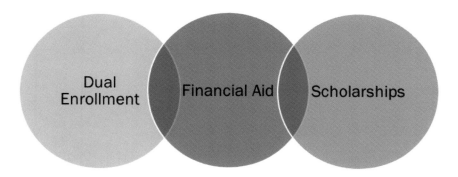

What Is Dual Enrollment?

It includes accelerated courses in high school that qualify toward BOTH high school diploma and college credits or career certificate.

To Qualify:

- College Credits: Students in grades 6-12, unweighted GPA of 3.0
- Career Certificate: Students in grades 6-12, unweighted GPA of 2.0
- Students must maintain the required GPA to stay qualified. Students must achieve a minimum score on common placement test.

How Does Dual Enrollment Benefit a Student?

- Studies show that students who participate in dual enrollment programs are more successful academically.
- College tuition and fees are waived for students in dual enrollment courses.
- Textbooks are loaned free-of-charge to students in public high school, resulting in significant savings.
- Students receive both college credit and credit towards high school graduation diploma.

- Challenge: Transportation to college campus to participate in classes.

What Is Financial Aid?

Financial aid is any grant, scholarship, or loan available to help students cover expenses related to college.

- Grants – Do not need to be repaid.
- Loans – Must be repaid at later date, with payments typically beginning upon graduation or withdrawal from college. Interest rates and repayment terms vary by loan program and should be reviewed carefully.
- The amount of financial aid a student receives is based upon state, federal, or institutional guidelines and other factors such as the cost of tuition and living expenses.

What Is the FAFSA?

The Free Application for Federal Student Aid (FAFSA) is a form that current and prospective college students should submit annually.

- Information provided on the FAFSA form is what federal, state, and institutional programs use to determine a student's eligibility for financial aid.
- The FAFSA is not typically required for private grants and scholarships.
- Students who file the FAFSA in October, November, or December receive more funding from federal, state, and college sources than students who file later in the year.

Why is the FAFSA important to fill out?

- Each year, approximately 50% of Florida high school seniors do not complete the FAFSA.

- Florida College Access Now (FCAN) estimates that high school graduates in Florida leave behind over $100 million in Pell Grants each year because they did not complete the FAFSA form.

- Students and their families should work with TSIC staff to get the support they need in completing their FAFSA forms.

What Is a Pell Grant?

A Pell Grant does not have to be repaid.

- The maximum Pell Grant is approximately $6,000. Go to https://studentaid.ed.gov/sa/types/grants-scholarships/pell for current maximums and other key information on Pell Grants.

- The amount awarded depends on financial need, cost to attend school, status as a full-time or part-time student, and plans to attend for a full academic year or less.
- To apply, students must submit a completed FAFSA form.
- Pell Grant funds are limited each year; early applicants are more likely to receive the total amount for which they qualify.

What Is a Scholarship?

- Scholarships are typically merit based.
- Scholarships do not require the student to pay back the funds at a later date.
- Scholarships are extremely competitive.
- Since many scholarships are only one year in length, they can be an unreliable source of financial aid.

What Types of Scholarships Are Available?

- **Traditional Scholarships:** Given to students to help pay for college tuition, they are awards that do not need to be repaid.
- **Alternative Scholarships:** Like traditional scholarships, these provide gifted or "free" money that does not require repayment. However, instead of helping cover tuition costs, alternative scholarships set very specific circumstances and criteria to qualify.

What Are Some Examples of Alternative Scholarships?

Emergency Scholarships: These alternative scholarships offer financial assistance for students facing unexpected hardship. The hardship must threaten the student's ability to persist or complete college. The scholarships are typically offered one time and are less than $1,500.

Performance-Based Scholarships: These alternative scholarships are financial aid for low-income students contingent upon completion of certain academic benchmarks. They are paid directly to students in multiple disbursements throughout the term and are intended to supplement other financial aid (federal and state).

Promise Scholarships: These alternative scholarships are institutional or place-based initiatives that offer funding for students who live in the program's geographic area. Some Promise Scholarships require completion of college prep programs, minimum GPA, specific attendance benchmarks, and/or completion of career plan.

Last Dollar In: These scholarships are intended to fill the gap between students' financial aid and the costs of college, such as computers, books and supplies, room and board, and even graduation expenses. "Last dollar in" scholarships are awarded to students whose official Expected Family Contribution (EFC), located on their Student Aid Report, and financial aid package totals are less than the cost of tuition and fees. "Last dollar in" scholarships vary greatly state to state.

Source: https://www.scholarships.com/financial-aid/college-scholarships/scholarships-by-type/last-dollar-scholarship/

Find and Apply for Scholarships
Step One—Evaluate your eligibility

- Many scholarships are merit-based, so start by determining which common criteria you meet.
- What is your GPA?
- Have you completed any college-level courses?

Step Two—Search

- Several scholarship search engines can help you find scholarships. These include Scholly, College Board's Scholarship Search, FastWeb, and Scholarships.com.
- Go for quantity – The more scholarships you apply for, the better are your chances for success. Develop a scholarship calendar that includes the deadlines for all the scholarships for which you plan to apply.

Step Three—Tell your story

- When writing essays for scholarships, find the stories you can share that demonstrate what makes you special.
- You should save all of your essays in order to re-use parts for other applications.
- Have a presentable presence on social media. Your online presence is part of your story.

Take Stock Innovation Collection: School-Based Approach

Take Stock in
Children®

The contents of this manual were developed under a grant from the U.S. Department of Education, Investing in Innovation (i3) Program. However, those contents do not necessarily represent the policy of the U.S. Department of Education, and you should not assume endorsement by the federal government.

Table of Contents

ACKNOWLEDGEMENTS

Take Stock in Children would like to thank and acknowledge the UNISON team for working tirelessly to launch and successfully implement the innovations supported by Take Stock in Children's Investing in Innovation (i3) grant. This team, led by Judy Saylor, Director of Program Growth and Innovation, includes Tiara Arline, Sara Buckley, Tiffany Givens, Amy Grunder, Roxanne Jordan, and Luz Rodriguez. The i3 grant program is ultimately about reaching scale — taking innovations from pilot to multiple sites and programs. Through the hard work of this team, these innovations will impact over 8,500 students per year through 45 independent affiliates across the Take Stock in Children network. Take Stock in Children would also like to thank the affiliate leadership who provided their experienced insight to better inform the development of this resource: Nancy Stellway (Palm Beach); Chuck Licis (Monroe); Kristin Carter (Duval/Putnam); Lisa Fasting (Pinellas); and Rachel Debigare (Alachua).

Finally, Take Stock in Children would like to recognize Gary Romano and the Civitas Strategies team for guiding the codification and scaling process of the innovations developed during the i3 grant program.

The increased number of students served, along with the continually growing demand, means that the UNISON innovations will provide the network with opportunities to more efficiently use resources, while still maintaining a high level of programmatic quality and service delivery. Scaling these elements will not only benefit the Take Stock in Children network but will also accelerate the progress of national scaling efforts. Network-wide adoption will effectively result in additional proof points and data, all of which will contribute to a climate conducive to national uptake.

Introduction

The Take Stock in Children model of support is built upon the foundation of the positive relationships students develop with their mentors. Field-based research has consistently proven the positive impact that a relationship with a caring adult can have on a student's academic and social-emotional development. There is strong evidence that a school-based mentoring approach is effective for decreasing drug and alcohol use, enhancing peer and parent-child relationships, increasing school attendance, and improving student attitudes about and performance in school (Tierney, Grossman, and Resch, 1995). These positive results are also illustrated by the outstanding results Take Stock in Children students continually demonstrate. Each Take Stock in Children student is matched with an adult mentor, who meets with the student at his/her school for an hour each week. Mentors provide academic and behavioral motivation, guidance, friendship, and support. This effective mentor support has greatly contributed to Take Stock in Children's annual results:

96% of Take Stock in Children students graduate high school on time

92% of Take Stock in Children students enter post-secondary education

68% of The Stock in Children Students complete post-secondary education, compared to the state average of 27% for at-risk students in poverty

The overall success of the program, along with the increasing number of students in need, has encouraged affiliates to prioritize growth in a concerted effort to increase the number of students served across the organization.

The school-based approach is one primary strategy that can be used to accelerate program growth and impact by pooling resources to maximize service level efficiency.

This strategy goes beyond traditional coordinated efforts and is particularly defined by the presence of a strong infrastructure, common agenda, and commitment to measurement. This is especially important in the school environment, where multiple partners may be working with the same students to achieve parallel goals.

The school-based approach is a strategy developed through Take Stock in Children's UNISON project, a federally funded Investing in Innovation (i3) grant, implemented at three school sites where Collective Impact was integrated into the implementation. The lessons learned from this project were instrumental in codifying the model for replication across the network. To provide further insight toward the development of the manual, Civitas Strategies conducted interviews with leadership staff from five Take Stock in Children affiliates who currently provide programming via variations of the school-based approach model: Alachua, Duval/Putnam, Monroe, Palm Beach, and Pinellas.

This manual is the result of that codification and will present information needed for launching and implementing the school- approach at your Take Stock in Children affiliate program.

Material covered in this manual includes the following:

- The definition of the school-based approach model;
- When to use a school-based approach;

- The benefits of the school-based approach;
- The challenges of the school-based approach and how to address them;
- Strategies for a school-based approach, including assessing readiness, designing and executing an action plan, and communicating for success; and
- Tools for implementation.

Launching a new program can be challenging, regardless of how comprehensive the instructions are. If you have any questions not covered in the manual or feedback that you would like to share, please contact the Take Stock in Children State Office

CHAPTER 1 Why Use a School-Based Approach?

Definition

The term "school-based approach" can have many definitions, depending on the audience. During this resource's development, we spoke with five different TSIC affiliates currently using variations of the school-based approach model.

For this manual's purpose, we will define "school-based approach" as a delivery model for providing students with college readiness services, characterized by four common elements:

1) The clustering of participating students at one or more strategically-chosen school sites;

2) Dedicated staff member(s) embedded at the site(s);

3) Effective engagement with school site leadership; and

4) A strong working partnership with the school district.

For detailed descriptions of the types of models that fit this profile, please see Choosing a Staffing Model.

Common Elements of the School-Based Approach

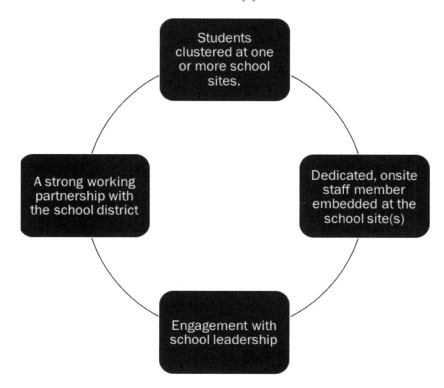

Benefits of the School-Based Approach

Sites piloting the school-based approach have reported many key benefits.

1. Maximization of internal resources to increase community impact	**2. Capacity for relationship-building**
3. Real-time support for students and mentors	**4. Greater community recognition**
5. Increased interaction with school personnel	

Benefit #1 – Maximization of internal resources to increase community impact. The most oft-stated reason that Take Stock in Children affiliates choose the school-based approach is that the clustering of students at a small number of school sites allows programs to maximize use of their available resources, including allocated money, program staff, and onboarded mentors. For example, a mentor may not have the time or flexibility to work with two students at schools located across town from one another; however, they may be able to work with additional students at the same school whom they can easily see during adjacent time slots. Similarly, college success coaches can often make more efficient use of their time if supporting students at 1-2 schools are located in close proximity, as opposed to at multiple sites across the county. In another example, it often proves more cost-effective (in terms of both time and money) to hold a college readiness workshop for a larger cohort of centralized students than to hold several sessions of the same workshop for smaller cohorts at multiple sites. By allowing program staff to make the most efficient use of available resources, the school-based approach can lead to increased numbers of student participants and greater overall impact to both the localized community and the county at-large.

Benefit #2 – Capacity for relationship-building. Besides the clustering of students, another key element of the school-based approach is the appointment of an embedded staff member or members, working primarily or exclusively onsite at the school campus. This practice allows the staff member to build stronger, more communicative relationships with the school's leadership and faculty. This can benefit the program in a myriad of ways, such as allowing program staff and classroom teachers to collaboratively address the needs of struggling students. Organizations using this approach have also found it much easier to learn the idiosyncrasies of working with school staff at 1-2 campuses than when the students they serve are spread out across many schools within the district or county.

Benefit #3 – Real-time support for students and mentors. Another benefit of having an embedded staff member onsite is the increased ability to provide on-the-spot, real-time support to students and mentors in need. For example, if a participating student has a troubling incident happen during the school day, such as a fight with a peer or a conflict with a teacher, the dedicated staff member is already on-site and has the flexibility to meet with the student immediately. Similarly, if a mentor encounters a scenario during a student session and needs guidance to address it effectively, an already present staff member can provide the needed support.

Benefit #4 – Greater community recognition. Several affiliates have reported that with their presence consolidated to several schools, as opposed to many across the district, they have come to be better known by community members, both internal (faculty, support staff, and unenrolled students) and external (families, community organizations, and local businesses). In turn, the increased awareness of TSIC's presence supports future recruitment and fundraising efforts.

Benefit #5 – Increased interaction with school personnel. One final benefit of the school-based approach is that this model naturally leads to increased interaction between affiliate staff and school personnel. This allows for greater communication between parties and helps affiliate staff to proactively — rather than reactively — address any program issues that arise.

Challenges of the School-Based Approach

Although the programs currently engaged in variations of the school-based approach agreed that there are extensive benefits to using this model, they also raised awareness of potential challenges that may arise during implementation.

1. Increased need for external resources	2. Potential for strained relationships with school staff
3. Increased need for program staff flexibility	4. Pressure to serve more sites

Challenge #1 – Increased need for external resources. While the school-based approach does allow for the maximization of internal resources (such as program staff), it can also place a greater strain on external resources, particularly the pool of potential mentors. The clustering of students that characterizes the school-based approach means that program staff may need to recruit a greater number of mentors, from a more restrictive geographic zone, to meet the need at the cluster school(s). This challenge may be particularly taxing for schools located in very rural areas or areas affected by seasonal population migration (i.e., people leaving Florida from the late spring to early fall), where the pool of potential mentors may already be depleted or diminished.

As a solution, programs may want to consider group mentoring as a means of matching more students with mentors.

Furthermore, by clustering students in more restricted geographic regions, there may be impact to the affiliate's ability to fundraise locally, if the chosen section of the county has many other organizations also vying for charitable dollars.

Challenge #2 – Potential for strained relationships with school staff. As mentioned, the school-based approach requires a strong working partnership between program staff and the faculty and administration at the cluster school(s). When these relationships are prioritized and nurtured, the school-based approach can flourish. However, if these relationships are not effectively maintained, challenges to model function can occur.

For example, some organizations reported that resentment can arise within school staff when external programs are allocated space and school resources when only a small percentage of the student population is being served. For example, school and program staff may need to share computers as well as copiers, and time constraints with these resources may cause friction. Furthermore, program and school staff relationships are particularly susceptible to change, especially at schools with high staff turnover. A carefully developed partnership between program and school staff can be severed if a key administrator or a large percentage of faculty leave unexpectedly during any given year.

Challenge #3 – Increased need for program staff flexibility. While the school-based approach boasts considerable potential for improving staff efficiency (see Benefit #1), it also requires program staff to remain flexible in the allocation of their time. For example, one organization noted that they cluster a large number of students at a school where administration has specifically requested that students are pulled only for staff check-ins during lunch or other non-academic periods.

In order to accommodate this request while also meeting the program model's requirement for individual, in-person check-ins, the program director occasionally needs to pull coaches assigned to other schools to complete this task. So, while efficiency is improved, programs considering this model may need to reset organizational expectations of assigned roles and responsibilities.

Challenge #4 – Pressure to serve more sites. Affiliates often feel pressure to serve greater numbers of sites so that service is distributed across districts and schools are not being left out. This pressure comes from a variety of stakeholders including principals, superintendents, community leaders, etc.

CHAPTER (2) Research

Despite the identified challenges, the programs we interviewed universally agreed that the benefits of using the school-based approach far outweigh any obstacles encountered. This perspective is further supported by research on the efficacy of school-based mentoring programs across the country.

In a 2014 report commissioned by MENTOR, the National Mentoring Partnership, researchers found that 1 in 3 American youth (or 16 million nationwide) report never having a mentor of any kind—either structured via a program like TSIC or naturally-occurring. Furthermore, this "mentoring gap" is even greater for at-risk youth. This statistic remains highly concerning, given that research has repeatedly shown that having a mentor greatly mitigates many of the risk factors present in these students' lives.

However, the National Mentoring Resource Center reports that school-based mentoring is one of the most efficient and cost-effective methods for both increasing the number of positive relationships students have in their lives, as well as boosting factors repeatedly shown to improve educational success, including connectedness with the school environment and academic self-confidence.

Equally significant is the type of students that school-based service programs tend to reach. A 2008 report by Education Northwest found that school-based mentoring programs consistently attract a pool of applicants who otherwise would not become involved with mentoring: namely, those typically served by community-based programs. Student participation in community-based mentoring programs is typically parent-initiated, whereas students participating in school-based programs are usually referred by a teacher or peer. Thus, students without a strong parental advocate are more likely to find the opportunity to participate in mentoring via a school-based program. The same report also cites numerous studies confirming that school-based programs are particularly effective for improving school-related outcomes, such as improved academic performance, improved self-perception of academic abilities, and a reduction in serious behavioral infractions and skipped classes.

CHAPTER 3 Launching a School-Based Approach

Overview of School-Based Approach Implementation

Three key phases prove key to implementing the school-based approach:

1. Define the Model;
2. Develop a Plan; and
3. Execute and Refine the Plan.

In "Define the Model," you will select the embedded staff and student service delivery models you plan to use. In "Develop a Plan," you will work through a series of planning steps to ensure your program is fully prepared for implementation. Finally, in "Execute and Refine the Plan," you will implement your designed model and refine as needed.

By the end of Year 1, the result will be a fully-established, school-based student service model. Each of these three phases is discussed in greater detail in the following section.

One important note: Before moving forward with planning a school-based approach model, take steps to ensure that all stakeholders, including district personnel and your affiliate board, agree with this decision. You may discover significant consequences to clustering services at certain schools; for example, depending upon budget constraints, it may mean eliminating the TSIC program from schools outside of the identified cluster. When considering adoption of this model, be sure everyone is aware and accepting of the potential benefits and consequences to your affiliate's specific situation.

Phases of Implementation for the School-Based Approach

Define the Model
- Choose a staffing model
- Choose a student service delivery model

Develop a Plan
- Determine the location
- Present a proposal
- Identify and acquire necessary resources
- Develop a timeline
- Establish a metric

Execute and Refine the Model
- Maintain a schedule
- Communicate regularly
- Track service delivery
- Reflect and make mid-course changes as needed
- Celebrate successes

Phase 1: Define the Model

The first step toward successfully implementing the school-based approach is to define the parameters of your program's ideal pilot model. In doing so, you must make decisions concerning the two models you will need: the staffing model and the student service delivery model.

District Employee	School Liaison	TSIC School-Based Employee
• Dedicated staff member at each school	• School staff member paid a stipend by your program to help coordinate onsite student services	• TSIC employee assigned to work onsite

Choose a Staffing Model:

As noted earlier in this manual, having a dedicated staff member or members embedded at the school site is an essential characteristic of the school-based approach. Below are three different types of staff members that programs have successfully used to implement their model, including the pros and cons identified for each type.

- The District Employee. One possibility is to contract with the local school district to employ a dedicated staff member at each of your identified cluster schools, either full- or part-time. This type of employee is hired and paid directly by the district but performs many of the responsibilities of a typical TSIC employee, such as providing college success coaching to students, facilitating workshops, and serving as a communications liaison between the program office and the school. Some programs have even chosen to contract their entire staff, including the program director, under the purview of the district.

  Pros: Having program staff employed by the school district may help eliminate much of the bureaucratic red tape that sometimes exists between programs and the district. Furthermore, district-employed TSIC staff can actively facilitate district-related tasks, such as providing access to students' academic data and collecting copies of free- or reduced-lunch letters.
  Cons: Program staff employed by the district may be beholden to districtwide policies that are not a good organizational fit; for example, one leader noted that their program's partnering school district requires employees to clock in a set number of hours during the work week, but does not account for the evening and weekend hours often required for the facilitation of TSIC program events.

Additionally, this option may not be available to all affiliates, particularly when working with a district that consistently experiences heavy financial constraints, or where staff availability shifts from year-to-year with budget fluctuations, causing program instability.

Affiliates with experience using this staff model also noted that using a district employee in the same capacity as an affiliate employee can present personnel complications; for example, the district employee may get paid a higher salary for essentially the same work, which can create discord among the affiliate staff.

- The School Liaison. The second option is to use school liaisons—that is, current staff members at the school who are paid a stipend by your program to help coordinate onsite student services. Organizations using this staffing model often recruit the school guidance counselor or volunteer coordinator to serve in this role, although teaching staff may be appropriate as well. Liaisons' tasks might include scheduling space for workshops, coordinating schedules and space for mentor-mentee meetings, and completing district liaison tasks, such as pulling copies of necessary student documents from their files. Some programs pay liaisons a flat fee for their service while others use a merit-based model based upon Balanced Scorecard Data.

Pros: Because the liaison is already a recognized member of the school faculty, the person in this role is uniquely positioned to help build effective partnerships between the program and the school. Liaisons are also well-situated to monitor student progress and communicate any major student concerns to program staff since they are onsite daily.

Cons: Because the school liaison has other full-time responsibilities for the school, he or she may not always have the time or flexibility to prioritize program-related tasks.

- The TSIC School-Based Employee. The third option is to assign a program employee—usually a College Success Coach—to work onsite at a specific cluster school(s). For this model to work effectively, it is imperative that the school-based program employee has a dedicated office space or conference room at the school. Although the primary base may be the affiliate home office, the school-based employee will ideally spend the majority of time onsite.

Pros: Coaches employed by the TSIC affiliate (as opposed to the district) may have more flexibility in how they implement their role because they are not restricted by district employee mandates.

Cons: Onsite program employees may experience some initial tension with school staff because they are not employed by the district. Several program leaders noted that at times, school faculty have expressed resentment that school-based TSIC employees are granted use of space and other resources within the school, even though they only serve a small percentage of the school's total student population. If choosing this model, program leadership should heavily emphasize the importance of relationship-building with their staff.

Experienced affiliates also noted that expectations and responsibilities can become muddled when a staff member is employed by the affiliate but working full-time in a school. It is critical to ensure that all stakeholders —the employee, the affiliate staff, and the school administration—are aligned on the parameters of the staff members' role. For example, the TSIC staff member shouldn't be required to fulfill other roles at the school unless specifically stated in the MOU (such as counseling students outside of the TSIC program or serving as advisor to a club where only a few TSIC students are members). Conversely, TSIC-employed staff members need to know whom to report to and when; for example, when planning workshops or campus tours, they should get approval from the school administration as well as their affiliate supervisor.

In our research with organizations currently employing the school-based approach, we determined that all three of these options can be effective for delivering high-quality student services to a large cohort of clustered students. Use Exercise 1 below to help determine which model is best suited to your organizational needs.

Choosing a Student Service Delivery Model:

Exercise 1: Choosing a Staffing Model — Your Best Fit for a Dedicated Staff Member

As a team, consider the following questions to help guide the decision-making process when determining the best staffing model for your program's school-based approach.

- What resources is the partnering district willing to provide? Are they able/willing to designate a staff member for TSIC service?
- What is your program's current relationship with the faculty and administration at the school you are considering? Are there staff who would be willing/interested in serving as TSIC liaisons?
- Does your affiliate currently have the capacity to designate individual staff members to a particular school site while still maintaining the rest of your program? Would you need to hire additional staff? Is this feasible to do?

In addition to one-to-one mentoring, college readiness coaching and the accompanying workshops are the hallmark of TSIC's success. The college success coach plays a significant role in the TSIC student's experience, both in introducing them to crucial readiness concepts and by providing regular face-to-face check-ins to gauge the student's current academic performance and physical/emotional well-being. Therefore, it is crucial to consider carefully how the college success coach will implement the program model with fidelity when working with a particularly large cohort of students at a cluster school. Organizations currently using the school-based approach generally fall into three categories of service delivery: The Club Model, the One-to-One Model, and the Hybrid Model.

- **The Club Model** – In this model, most or all of the interactions between the embedded staff member and the students occur in a group setting. Students are divided into one or more "clubs," depending upon the cohort's size. The staff member will then meet with each club on a regularly scheduled basis, either after school or during a common free time in the students' school schedule, to discuss relevant topics, provide well-being check-ins, and problem-solve any issues members of the club are experiencing. For programs attempting to host very large cohorts, the club model may be the most efficient means of providing services to all students.

- **The One-to-One Model** – In this model, the college success coach regularly meets with each student in the school cohort for one-to-one coaching sessions. Several affiliate staff members expressed that this model is their ideal scenario, stating that one-to-one sessions are essential for relationship-building between the coach and the student; this model also allows the coach to provide a more personalized session

to the student's particular needs. However, it may not always be financially or logistically possible to staff a large cohort so that every student frequently receives one-to-one coaching sessions.

- **The Hybrid Model** – The majority of affiliates interviewed stated that their program uses a hybrid of the Club and One-to-One models; that is, college success coaches hold some group sessions but also aim for at least half of their student check-ins throughout the year to happen individually. Some affiliates have created versions of the hybrid model that are adapted to the specific needs of their school. For example, one TSIC affiliate described staff setting up informal "office hours" at a table outside the cafeteria several times a month, which allows coaches to briefly touch base with most students as they pass by and also gives students the opportunity to engage one-on-one if needed. This variation on the hybrid may be particularly effective at schools where students cannot be pulled out of class for check-ins or where after-school meetings are challenging because of extracurricular activities.

Use the questions in Exercise 2 below to help determine which service delivery model is right for your organization.

Exercise 2: Choosing a Service Delivery Model

As a team, consider the following questions to help guide the decision-making process when determining the best student service delivery model for your program's school-based approach.

- What are the minimum service delivery requirements for TSIC that must be accounted for in this plan? What is the ideal? How do they compare?
- What resources (staffing, dedicated space) will be needed to carry out the service delivery model you are planning? Are these resources you have at your disposal or will you need to acquire them?

Once you have determined the location for implementation (see page 16), you will also want to consider the following:

- Are there any location-specific limitations that need to be considered? For example, if the principal will not allow students to be pulled from class, coaches would need to plan for meeting during lunch or after school.

Phase 2: Develop a Plan

Once you have defined the scope of your model, the next step is to develop a plan for implementation. To streamline this process, we have broken the planning process into five steps:

1. Determine the Location, 2. Present a Proposal, 3. Identify & Acquire Necessary Resources, 4. Develop a Timeline, and 5. Establish a Metric to Indicate Success.

The 5-Step Planning Process

| Step 1: Determine the Location | Step 2: Present a Proposal | Step 3: Identify & Acquire Necessary Resources | Step 4: Develop a Timeline | Step 5: Establish a Metric to Indicate Success |

Step One: Determine the Location

There are a number of factors to consider when determining the location(s) at which you will pilot the school-based approach. Use Exercise 3 below to help you assess the appropriateness of locations you may be considering.

Exercise 3: Determining the Ideal Pilot Location

As a team, consider the following factors to determine the ideal school site for piloting the school-based approach.

- **Feeder Patterns** – Where have the majority of your affiliate's student participants come from? Are you more likely to find greater numbers of eligible students in a particular section of the county or neighborhood?

- **Successful Track Record** – At which school(s) does your affiliate already have a successful track record of helping students graduate from high school and enter post-secondary programs? The affiliates surveyed universally agreed that it is easier to expand a previously established program than to begin by clustering students at a new site.

- **Geographic Accessibility** – If planning to pilot the school-based approach at more than one location, it may prove important to select school sites in close proximity to one another to best maximize staff usage.

- **Mentor Availability** – Is the site(s) you are considering in an area with sufficient potential for recruiting mentors? Expansion of the student cohort means a greater need for mentors, so consider piloting the school-based approach in close proximity to businesses and other organizations where mentor recruitment efforts are likely to be successful, such as at a large local corporation or college campus.

- **Donor Interest** – Is there an area of the county where donors have expressed particular interest in funding? Some affiliates noted that donors are often interested in giving to a particular community or neighborhood. If this is true in your region, it may be important to consider schools located within that area to expand potential fundraising opportunities.

- **Engaged Administration and Faculty** – How interested and/or engaged with TSIC's mission are the staff at the school site(s) you are considering? Multiple affiliates noted this as the most important consideration when determining where to pilot the school-based approach.

Step Two: Present the Proposal

Once you have determined the ideal location(s) for piloting the school-based approach, you will need to present your proposed model to the relevant partners—the school district and leadership at the selected school(s). One important consideration: district personnel may have their own thoughts about where they would like to see TSIC services begin or expand. Furthermore, they may have identified schools other than the ones your team has carefully selected in accordance with the criteria listed in the previous exercise. While a strong working partnership with the district is crucial to implementation, it is equally important that affiliates do consider the above criteria when making a final location determination. Program leaders cited several scenarios where they had selected schools for program expansion based solely on district recommendation, only to discover that the school's leadership was not interested in engaging the program's services for their students. Therefore, it is extremely important to do your own due diligence in assessing the school leadership's interest level in partnering with TSIC before committing to a location. The importance of buy-in from school leadership at a school-based program site cannot be overstated.

Expert Tip

Expert Tip: It is highly recommended to do your own research when determining the best site for clustering students. District recommendation should be a key factor, but it is critical to assess whether you will have buy-in from the school's administration and faculty.

A multitude of benefits to having the support of your school-based site's administration are evident. These may include the following: invitations to attend school events (extremely useful toward student recruitment efforts); assistance with recruiting faculty members to serve as school ambassadors or mentors; and a commitment to consistently maintain a dedicated space for TSIC staff to work within the school building. Conversely, affiliates reported that it is extremely difficult to successfully implement the school-based approach at a site where school leaders are indifferent to, or even resentful of, TSIC's presence at the school. Therefore, if compromise with the district is required for your proposal's acceptance, it may become necessary to prioritize the engagement level of the school leaders over other considerations.

As noted, it is extremely important when discussing a model type with district and school personnel to outline very clear role responsibilities for the school staff member, whether employed by the district or affiliate. All stakeholders should be in agreement on the embedded staff member's responsibilities, as well as from whom to garner approval when planning job-related activities and events.

See Attachment A for a template outlining the information to include in a proposal to district/school leadership.

Once your program and the district have reached an agreement as to the selection of the site(s) and the type of model to implement, all aspects of the proposed partnership, including goals, infrastructure, roles, and responsibilities, should be codified in a memorandum of understanding (MOU) signed by both partners. This crucial step helps ensure everyone's expectations for Year One of implementation are aligned. (Please note: Before attempting to develop an MOU, please check with district personnel — they may have a standard template they prefer to use).

Similarly, if you are planning to pay stipends to school or district personnel serving in an ambassador role, it is important to sign a Stipend Agreement with the liaison. Be aware that if the stipend is over a prescribed amount ($600 at the time of this manual's publication), the liaison may need to be made aware of tax implications.

- See Attachment B for a protocol on constructing an MOU.
- See Attachment C for a sample MOU.
- See Attachment D for a sample Stipend Agreement.

Please note: This section is not intended as legal advice. It is always advised to consult with legal counsel when entering into a new contract.

Step Three: Identify & Acquire Necessary Resources

Once your proposal has been accepted and your pilot site(s) selected, you will need to analyze your existing resources and perform a needs assessment to determine what your program will need to secure or acquire to implement the model. Use the questions in the exercise on the next page to begin brainstorming potential needs; then use the template in Attachment E to record your findings.

Exercise 4: Needs-Based Assessment:

As a team, consider the following questions to assess your existing and needed resources for the proposed model.

Staffing:

- Given the number of students you intend to add, how many additional mentors will you need to recruit?
- If using the School Ambassador model, how many ambassadors will you need to recruit?
- If using the School-Based TSIC employee model, how many college success coaches will you need to recruit?
- Are there any new or additional positions you will need to recruit for and fill to implement the model effectively? Examples might include support staff to expand administrative capacity or a part-time fundraiser to assist with raising the funds necessary to support an expanded model.

Dedicated Space:

- Has leadership at the selected school(s) designated a dedicated space for TSIC services?
- If so, does the dedicated space have the following:
- Room for any anticipated activities, including cohort meetings
- Access to electricity
- Ability to ensure privacy
- Provisions for any necessary technology (internet hookups or WIFI, etc.)

Resources & Supplies:

- Do affiliate staff currently have TSIC system-enabled laptop computers to use when working onsite?
- Is the school supplying the furniture (desks, chairs, couch, etc.) for the dedicated space or will the affiliate need to provide?
- Is the school supplying the technology (phones, printers, copier, etc.) for the dedicated space or will the affiliate need to provide?
- What training materials will need to be created/updated to prepare staff for the expansion and/or develop any new staff?
- Any other resources or supplies needed?

Step Four: Create an Implementation Timeline

The next step is to develop a timeline of the tasks and events that will need to occur as part of the implementation process. The timeline will prescribe both the sequence of tasks and the corresponding due dates, as well as the party responsible. Ideally, the timeline will map out all important tasks and events throughout the first year of implementation. To begin this step, use the questions outlined in Exercise 5 below. Use the template in Attachment F to record and map the results

Exercise 5: Creating a Timeline for Year One of Implementation

As a team, brainstorm a list of events and tasks that need to occur before and during Year One implementation. When developing the list, consider the following questions:

- What positions (paid and volunteer) do you need to recruit for? When do you plan to begin the recruitment period? When do all hires need to be completed by?
  - Additional Mentors
  - Additional College Success Coaches
  - School Ambassadors (if using this model)
  - Administrative Support
  - Mentor Coordinator
  - Fundraising Support
- How many new students do you plan to enroll in the program? When does the student recruitment period begin/end? When does the application review period begin/end?
- When do you plan to have new students inducted into the program by?
- Are there any upcoming school or community events where recruitment efforts could take place?
- Are there any upcoming community events where fundraising and outreach efforts could take place?
- Are there any upcoming school events where dedicated staff members could be introduced to school faculty and leadership? If not, can you plan one?
- When can the dedicated campus space be set up for TSIC use?
- When will new staff training take place?
- Are there any kick-off events planned for students and/or mentors at the start of the school year?
- When will mentor-mentee matches be notified that they have been matched?
- When should mentoring sessions begin/end?

- When should college success coaching sessions begin/end?
- When do student check-ins (group or individual) begin/end?
- When do you anticipate college readiness workshops occurring?
- When do you anticipate college tours or educational field trips occurring?
- Are there mid- or end-of-year celebrations planned?
- Are there additional trainings staff will need throughout the year

Note: For some of these events, it will be important to get approval from school leadership. Remember that a little consideration goes a long way toward building effective working relationships, so considering the needs of the school when selecting dates for the timeline is important. For example, unless school leadership indicates otherwise, it is best to avoid planning events during the first and last weeks of school, as well as the days immediately preceding and during standardized testing. Obtaining a copy of the school's calendar before attempting a timeline is highly recommended!

The interviewed TSIC affiliates emphasized the importance of planning for the increase in capacity required of all staff positions when expanding your program to a school-based approach. For example, one program found it necessary to hire a mentor coordinator because their school-specific college success coaches no longer had the capacity to manage the scheduling and recruitment efforts required to manage the mentoring component. Another affiliate is looking to hire an additional administrative assistant to handle the influx of paperwork that comes with increasing the size of a student cohort.

Step Five: Establish a Metric to Indicate Success

The last step before implementation is to craft a set of 3–5 metrics to define and evaluate success in Year One of implementation. Each metric should be SMART (Specific, Measurable, Achievable, Relevant, and Timebound), and should be agreed upon by all relevant stakeholders, including embedded staff, affiliate leadership, and school leadership, as appropriate. For example: "The student cohort will achieve a 95% school attendance rate, with no participating student falling below 92%, by the end of the school year."

Consider setting metrics in any of the following arenas:

- Student attendance
- Average student grade point average (GPA)
- Average number of mentoring sessions held (should be above the TSIC requirement)
- Average number of staff check-ins held per student
- Number of college readiness workshops provided (should be above the TSIC requirement)
- Number of club meetings held (if using the Club model)
- Number of new mentors recruited
- Number of additional dollars raised (including by what means)
- Number of grants applied for
- Number of students recruited for Year One of implementation
- Percentage of growth in students recruited for Year Two of implementation

Phase 3: Execute and Refine the Model

With the plan in place, it is time to put it into action. We have identified five critical steps to successfully execute and, when necessary, refine the model. The embedded staff member should play the critical role in facilitating each step to ensure the project stays on track.

Here are the five key steps: 1. Maintain a Schedule of Meetings and Activities, as indicated by the timeline, 2. Communicate Regularly About Successes and Challenges, 3. Track Service Delivery, 4. Reflect and Make Mid-Course Changes in Response to Data Collected, and 5. Celebrate Successes. The embedded staff member monitors progress and keeps services on track following the steps in the following figure.

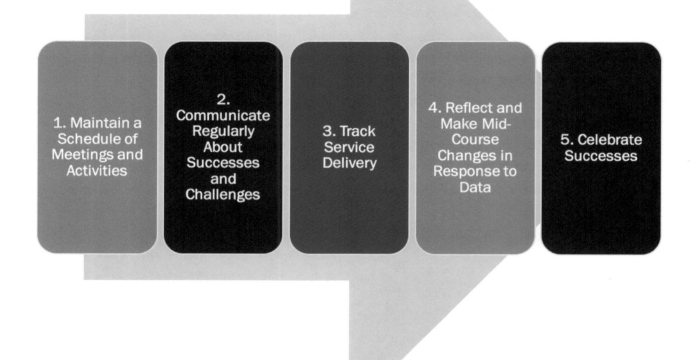

Step One: Maintain a Schedule of Meetings and Activities

Beginning with the timeline you have already created, develop a schedule of all relevant activities and meetings for the year ahead. This is also the time to make any necessary determinations on how often the embedded staff member will meet with students (as a group and/or individually), which should be noted as well. The embedded staff member has the responsibility of ensuring that all relevant stakeholders (including school leadership) have a copy of the schedule. The staff member should also take responsibility for sending reminders to attendees (students, school staff, and program staff) prior to all events and ensuring that any necessary event space is secured and approved for use well in advance.

Going forward, it is recommended to schedule a start-of-school planning meeting to ensure all stakeholders are aware of and aligned on expectations and responsibilities.

Step Two: Communicate Regularly About Successes and Challenges

The most critical path of communication is between program leadership and the embedded staff member. Since the staff member will be mostly onsite (even if technically working from the program office), it is crucial that regular check-ins are scheduled at least monthly (if not weekly) to update and track the implementation progress made and to brainstorm solutions to any challenges encountered. It will be equally important to document these conversations to ensure that appropriate programmatic "tweaks" are made in accordance with lessons learned throughout the year. At times, it may be appropriate to invite school and/or district leadership to these meetings as well, especially when any challenges or logistical decisions to be made are directly tied to the school environment. On the flipside, school leaders will also appreciate being kept abreast of program successes; consider establishing a means of regularly communicating these to school and district leaders as a means of further developing the working partnership between them and your program. Possibilities might include sending a monthly email update on implementation progress or inviting them to attend celebratory events such as your end-of-year celebration.

EXPERT TIP

Because the embedded staff member is mostly working outside of the affiliate office, staff communications will rely more heavily on technology (email, phone conferences, etc.). It can be very helpful to establish a common folder or drive for keeping required data, documents, etc., that all staff can access easily from remote locations.

Step Three: Track Service Delivery

Before the school year starts, it is important to develop a system for tracking the delivery of student services: mentoring sessions, coaching sessions, staff-student check-ins, workshops held, etc. If your program has a standardized system already in place, ensure that embedded staff members are trained and practiced in using it, as well as fully aware of what their responsibilities are in terms of monitoring service delivery. Ensure that in addition to required program data, the embedded staff member is also tracking any data relevant to the metrics previously established and agreed-upon by stakeholders. This data should be reviewed by both the embedded staff member and program leadership on a monthly basis to ensure the model is on track and determine if any intervention is necessary.

Step Four: Reflect and Make Mid-Course Changes in Response to the Data

The data collected in Step Three should be reviewed by both the embedded staff member and program leadership on at least a monthly basis to ensure that the model is on track and determine if any intervention is necessary. Expect that some trial and error will occur, as it is a natural part of the process when implementing a new initiative. One organization we spoke with originally intended to use the Club model exclusively to serve students but found upon implementation that their student drop-out rate began to rise. When they changed course to include more opportunities for one-to-one staff-student check-ins, their program completion rate began to rebound. Components of the model that work well at one school site may not work at another; thus, the process of regularly reflecting upon the data is the key to a successful program.

It is also recommended to schedule an end-of-school-year reflection meeting with all stakeholders, to assess overall progress and inform future planning.

Step Five: Celebrate Successes

As noted above, it is always important to reflect upon and celebrate successes that occur. The embedded staff member should also take responsibility for ensuring the progress made is well-documented and broadly communicated to all stakeholders. If they are not already included on the timeline, be sure to plan some celebratory events throughout the year so that students, their families, and their mentors can join staff in honoring the progress made throughout Year One!

An Additional Note on Building Relationships with Key Partners:

As noted several times throughout this manual, the development of an effective school-based model is virtually impossible without the support and cooperation of the key partners: namely, the school district and the school's leadership team. It is imperative that program leadership prioritize the development of positive working relationships with these stakeholders and coach their staff to do the same. It is inevitable that the needs of the school and the program will occasionally be at odds; thus, it is important to remember at all times that both parties are committed to the same mission: positive, foundational outcomes for students. As external partners, it is crucial that program staff recognize that the scope of their programmatic agenda is relatively narrow, while school leaders are beholden to the needs of many—students, faculty and staff, parents, the teachers' union, district personnel, and the Board of Education. The more accommodating and supportive of the school leadership's agenda the program can be, the better the odds of reciprocation. To this end,

the following is a list of suggestions gleaned from the experience of programs currently practicing the school-based approach:

- Invite school and district leadership to attend (or even speak) at important program events such as the kickoff celebration and end-of-year awards ceremony.
- Consider inviting school or district personnel to join your affiliate board of directors. This can be a great way to ensure strong communication and collaboration between parties.
- Do not be a drain on school resources; assume the affiliate should provide any necessary supplies (use of a copier and printer, reams of paper, desk supplies, etc.) for the dedicated staff member, unless otherwise indicated.

- Encourage dedicated staff to prioritize building relationships with school faculty in addition to school administrators. Some may be willing to serve as mentors while others might aid recruitment efforts by highlighting the TSIC mission with students and families.
- Provide professional development trainings in effective communication and collaboration skills to all affiliate staff, including dedicated staff assigned to a specific school.
- Share student successes with school and district leadership; ensure that they are included in any network

communications such as monthly newsletters.

- Be polite, be respectful, be humble—remember that you are a guest on their turf (even if for the sake of providing an invaluable service to their students!).

Conclusion

There is no doubt that the school-based approach requires very careful consideration and thoughtful planning in order to achieve successful implementation and sustainability. However, review of both the scholarly research and interviews with TSIC affiliate leadership has repeatedly shown that when implemented with fidelity, the advantages of the school-based approach far outweigh the challenges your program may face along the way. Your staff will appreciate the efficiency and school familiarity this model allows, and most importantly, the expansion will allow your program to serve more students without decreasing the quantity or quality of the services provided. We hope that the tools and collective wisdom gathered in this manual will help you develop a program approach that best serves the needs of your students. Furthermore, we hope to see this manual grow dynamically as more affiliates work toward implementation of the school-based model. As you work toward adoption of the approach, please share any lessons learned or helpful tools with the State Office so we can continue to update this manual accordingly.

CHAPTER 4 — Frequently Asked Questions (FAQs)

Q: My program is located in a rural county, and we already struggle to recruit mentors. What are your suggestions for expanding the recruitment pool?

A: Remember that clustering students at 1-2 schools may allow current mentors to easily add additional students to their roster. Also, by increasing your organizational presence at a specific school, your program may be better placed to recruit school staff to serve. You could also consider recruiting at some of the prominent businesses, government agencies, and organizations in your locale, such as the county sheriff's office and/or police department, the local hospital, nearby churches, the local elementary school, college campuses, and civic organizations (e.g., the Rotary Club, the Elks, etc.).

Q: Is it advised to pilot the school-based approach at a school with an existing TSIC cohort or at a new school interested in adding a TSIC program?

A: The affiliate staff we interviewed generally agreed that programs interested in piloting the school-based approach are better off expanding an existing program, rather than starting from scratch at a new site. The benefits are that the TSIC program is already well-known to staff, students, and families, which should help with efforts to recruit new participants (both students and staff mentors). An exception to this rule is if the existing site's administration has not historically been supportive of your program in the past. As noted throughout this manual, school leadership and staff buy-in is crucial to the success of the school-based approach; therefore, in this situation it may be advisable to select a new site where leadership is more enthusiastic about your program.

Q: If I cluster the TSIC students in my county, what happens when we receive an application from a student not at a cluster school?

A: One of the downsides to the school-based approach may be that you sometimes have to reject a qualified student's application because he or she does not attend a cluster school. That said, several interviewees noted finding "work-arounds" for this issue. For example, if the student attends a school geographically close to or affiliated with the cluster school, it may be possible to include the student in this program; if a middle school student is on the same campus as the cluster high school, the embedded staff member may be able to coordinate services to include this participant relatively easily. If this is not possible due to the distance between schools, the affiliate staff we spoke with recommended keeping an updated list of local organizations that provide similar mentoring and/or college readiness services to provide to these students.

ATTACHMENT A

Program Proposal Template

Lead Contact at the Program (include contact info):

Lead Contact at the District or School (include contact info):

Proposed Location(s) for Implementation of the Model:

Proposed Model of Student Service Delivery (include what services the program will provide, the number of students served, and the frequency of service):

Resources and Support Provided by the Program:

Resources and Support Provided by the District/School:

Timing (include start and end dates for each location proposed):

ATTACHMENT B

Developing an MOU

Please note: This section is not intended as legal advice. It is always advised to consult with legal counsel when entering into a new contract.

A Memorandum of Understanding (MOU) is designed to outline expectations. Regardless of the level of collaboration, it is important to outline the roles that each party will play in building a partnership between TSIC and the school district. The MOU can serve as an important tool to guide future meetings, check in on progress, and make adjustments based on past learning. Use the information compiled by using this guide and the other appendices, and make sure to include the following:

1. Partnership objectives
   a. What goals is this MOU designed to facilitate?
   b. What staffing model is your program proposing to use?
2. Communication
   a. Who are the point people from each organization?
   b. How often will the point people meet?
   c. What method of communication will be used in between face-to-face contact?
3. Program structure
   a. What student service model is your program proposing to use?
   b. What staffing model is your program proposing to use? Whose human resource policies will the embedded staff member(s) follow?
   c. What are the responsibilities of the TSIC affiliate in delivering the model?
   d. What are the responsibilities of the district/school in delivering the model?
   e. What are the responsibilities of the embedded staff member?
   f. Who will the embedded staff member report to?
   g. Who is responsible for programmatic decision-making? In what circumstances do both parties need to be involved?
4. Evaluation
   a. What metrics will be measured?
   b. What tools will be used to measure these metrics?
   c. What data will be shared? How often?
   d. Who will analyze the data?
5. Funding
   a. What are the financial responsibilities of the district/school?
   b. What are the financial responsibilities of the TSIC affiliate?
   c. Have all responsibilities been approved by the appropriate personnel?

6. Ending the partnership

    a.   Are there any reasons the partnership might end? What are they?

    b.   What is th e process to discontinue the partnership?

See also the sample MOU, Attachment C.

ATTACHMENT C

Sample MOU

Sample Memorandum of Understanding (MOU)
Between TSIC and XXX School District

It is considered a best practice for a Take Stock in Children affiliate and its district partner to sign a Memorandum of Understanding (MOU). An MOU outlines roles, responsibilities, and expectations, and helps strengthen partnerships.

The following is a sample MOU that illustrates the areas that partners might wish to include in their agreement. Affiliates should edit this to align to their unique situation.

This Memorandum of Understanding (MOU) is entered into by and between the following entities: _____ and _____.

These entities are partnering to support students enrolled in the Take Stock in Children (TSIC) intervention. TSIC provides a unique opportunity for deserving low-income students to escape the cycle of poverty via higher education. The program offers students post-secondary scholarships, caring volunteer mentors, and hope for a better life. The comprehensive services start in middle school, continue through high school, and include students' transition into post-secondary education.

I. Scope of Work

Each group applicant agrees to participate in the proposed partnership and work collaboratively toward the shared goals. These goals include the following:

Insert goals and objectives as determined during group discussion

II. Joint Responsibilities for Communications and Development of Timelines

Each group understands that ongoing and consistent communication is necessary for a strong partnership in service of students' success.

1) Each member of the group will appoint a key contact person for this partnership.

2) These key contacts will maintain frequent communication to facilitate cooperation under this MOU.

3) These key contacts will work together to determine needs and to provide project updates and status reports.

The point person/people for _____ are: _____

The point person/people for _____ are: _____

Regular communication will take place via insert frequency and type of meetings.

III. Responsibilities

A number of events and activities will structure the partnership. Both partners will play important roles in making sure these are a success and help advance the mission. Each party agrees to the following responsibilities:

TSIC will be responsible for the following: insert responsibilities

Partner will be responsible for the following: insert responsibilities

IV. Evaluation and Data Sharing

The partners have agreed to the following metrics to assess progress toward goals:

Insert agreed upon metrics

To measure these outcomes, each partner will agree to collect and share the following information:

TSIC will insert data sharing responsibilities

Partner will insert data sharing responsibilities

V. Fiscal Responsibility

Insert any information regarding fiscal responsibility

VI. Working Relationship Among Group Members

The following guidelines will be followed to ensure partners uphold their responsibilities:

To be filled in according to the members' agreement and the project's design. This section might address the members' agreement on the steps to be taken in the event one member is not fulfilling its responsibilities.

VII. Modifications

This MOU may be amended only by written agreement signed by each of the group members. A formal review of the MOU will occur annually, at which point partners will assess successes and challenges and set priorities for the coming year.

VIII. Effective Date/Duration/Termination

This MOU shall be effective beginning with the date of the last signature hereon. It will be reviewed each year, and modifications can be made at that time. In the event that one partner wants to discontinue the partnership, they will request a meeting with the other partner for information sharing. The ending of the partnership will be put into writing, with each party agreeing to fulfill any final responsibilities that work in service of the students.

Insert any pre-defined reasons for ending partnership

IX Signatures

1) TSIC Affiliate

_____

Signature/Date

_____

Print Name/Title/Name of Affiliate

2) Higher Education Partner Representative

_____

Signature/Date

_____

Print Name/Title/Name of Institution

ATTACHMENT D

Take Stock in Children
Sample Stipend Agreement

This agreement is between Take Stock in Children, hereafter "TSIC", and X, who has agreed to serve as the school liaison for X High School for the TSIC program. The liaison will be considered an Independent Contractor for TSIC, and a W9 Form must be completed.

Duties:

The duties of the liaison include the following: (list duties)

Compensation:

The liaison will be compensated $X for the X school year. Payment will be made in X installments, directly to the school liaison. Liaison should submit Invoice for Services

Performed.

• First installment ($X) will be paid at the end of the first semester.

• Second installment ($X) will be paid at the end of the X school year.

Agreement:

I,_____ agree to the terms above to be the X High School Take Stock in Children X school liaison.

_____
Signature

_____
Date

_____
Principal Name

_____
Date

_____
Principal Signature

_____
Take Stock in Children Executive Director

_____
Date

Please note: If the stipend exceeds $600, there may be tax implications for the payee. Please be advised.

ATTACHMENT E

Needs-Based Assessment

Resource	Have	Will Need:	Plan for Acquiring/ Purchasing:
Staffing:			
Mentors:			
College Success Coaches			
School Ambassadors			
Administrative:			
Fundraising:			
Other Staff:			
Supplies:			
Laptop Computers:			
Desktop Computers			
Printers:			
Other:			
Computer Equipment:			
Software:			
Office Supplies:			
Curriculum:			
:Dedicated Space			
Desks:			
Chairs:			
Other Furniture:			
Miscellaneous:			

ATTACHMENT F:

Timeline Template

Event/Task	Date Range	Location	Person Responsible
Example: Recruit for part-time Administrative Assistant to assist with addition of 50 student applications and 20 new mentors.	Begin May 1st Needs to be completed by June 30th	Interviews held at Affiliate Office	Program Director, assisted by current administrative Assistant

Be Sure to Include:

- Staff Recruitment
- Student Recruitment
- Staff Training
- Student Induction

- Program Kickoff
- Workshops
- School/Community Events
- End-of-Year Celebration

Take Stock
Innovation Collection:
Post-Secondary Partnership
Approach

Take Stock in
Children®

The contents of this manual were developed under a grant from the U.S. Department of Education, Investing in Innovation (i3) Program. However, those contents do not necessarily represent the policy of the U.S. Department of Education, and you should not assume endorsement by the federal government.

Table of Contents

ACKNOWLEDGEMENTS

Take Stock in Children would like to thank and acknowledge the UNISON team that has tirelessly worked to launch and successfully implement the innovations supported by Take Stock in Children's Investing in Innovation (i3) grant. This team, led by Judy Saylor, Director of Program Growth and Innovation, includes Tiara Arline, Sara Buckley, Tiffany Givens, Amy Grunder, Roxanne Jordan, and Luz Rodriguez. The i3 grant program is ultimately about reaching scale—taking innovations from pilot to multiple sites and programs. Through the hard work of this team, these innovations will impact over 8,500 students per year through 45 independent affiliates across the Take Stock in Children network.

Take Stock in Children would also like to thank the affiliate leadership who provided their experienced insight to better inform the development of this resource: Judi Zanetti & Meaghan Magmoll (Marion), Betty Safiotti (Indian River), Kelly Astro (Orange), Connie Kolisnyk & Carman Cullen-Batt (Lake/Sumter), and Amanda Frey (Broward).

Finally, Take Stock in Children would like to recognize Gary Romano, Alison LaRocca, and the Civitas Strategies team for guiding the codification and scaling process of the innovations developed during the i3 grant program.

The increased number of students served along with a continually growing demand means that the UNISON innovations will provide the network with opportunities to efficiently use resources as well as maintain a high level of programmatic quality and service delivery. Scaling these elements will not only benefit the Take Stock in Children network but will also accelerate the progress of national scaling efforts. Network-wide adoption will effectively result in additional proof points and data, all which will contribute to a climate conducive to national uptake.

Introduction

The Take Stock in Children model of support is built upon the positive relationships that students develop with their mentors. The impact that a caring adult can have on a student's academic and social-emotional development has been proven in field-based research. There is strong evidence that a school-based mentoring approach decreases drug and alcohol use, enhances peer and parent-child relationships, increases school attendance, and improves attitudes about and performance in school (Tierney, Grossman and Resch, 1995). These positive results are also illustrated in the outstanding results of Take Stock in Children students. Each Take Stock in Children student is matched with a caring adult mentor who meets with the student at his/her school for an hour each week. Mentors provide academic and behavioral motivation, guidance, friendship, and support. This effective mentor support has greatly contributed to Take Stock in Children's results:

96% of Take Stock in Children students graduate high school on time

92% of Take Stock in Children students enter post-secondary education

68% of The Stock in Children Students complete post-secondary education, compared to the state average of 27% for at-risk students in poverty

The overall success of the program, along with the increasing number of students in need, have encouraged affiliates to target growth in an effort to increase the number of students served across the organization.

Partnering with post-secondary institutions can magnify growth and impact by better equipping students for their post-secondary experience. It is a mutually beneficial strategy, which also serves the goals of colleges and universities to recruit and retain students. The purpose of this manual is to provide a blueprint for affiliates who would like to deepen their relationships with a post-secondary program or institution in their area. Many affiliates seeking to build such partnerships will do so with higher learning institutions (i.e., local colleges and universities). However, this manual intentionally references "post-secondary partnerships" as some may be looking to collaborate with local vocational programs as well.

This strategy can be implemented along a continuum, ranging from informal partnerships based on individual relationships to codified agreements with shared staffing. Initial evaluation about similar programs point to students' increased college readiness and even retention when these types of partnerships are in place.

The Take Stock in Children Post-Secondary Partnership Model is an evolving strategy, informed by existing programs and research. This strategy has been identified as a critical way to strengthen the program moving forward and will be prioritized at the state level.

The Post-Secondary Partnership Manual is the result of research around best practices and will present information intended to help Take Stock in Children affiliates assess their partnership activities and determine next steps. The purpose of the partnership model and the guidelines presented in this manual are designed to help local affiliates forge relationships with local post-secondary institutions to benefit the middle and high school students they serve.

Material covered in this manual includes the following elements, all focused on serving students in middle school and high school:

- The definition of post-secondary institution partnerships;
- Research about post-secondary/ nonprofit partnerships;
- Qualities of TSIC partnerships with post-secondary institutions;
- Steps for creating a post-secondary partnership;
- Rubric to assess intensity of post-secondary partnerships; and
- Attachments with resources to support moving forward toward collaboration.

Launching any new program can be challenging, regardless of the depth of the instructions. If you have any questions not covered in the manual or feedback in general you would like to share, please contact the Take Stock in Children State Office.

CHAPTER (1) Why Partner with Post-Secondary Institutions?

Definition of Partnership

Partnerships between Take Stock in Children and local post-secondary institutions (such as colleges and universities) will vary based on community needs and leadership but will also share the common goal of better preparing students for post-secondary success. They also share the following elements:

- Supplement students' academic studies with lessons that familiarize them with post-secondary culture as well as the financial aid process;
- Include events and workshops on college campuses, partly geared to expose middle and high school students to that environment;
- Require ongoing communication between the post-secondary institution and TSIC;
- Allow for data sharing between post-secondary institution and TSIC—in compliance with the Family Educational Rights and Privacy Act (FERPA); and
- Are mutually beneficial, increasing student preparedness as well as post-secondary institution recruitment.

Benefits of Post-Secondary Partnerships

Sites that have successfully partnered with post-secondary institutions have reported a myriad of benefits:

- Students gain familiarity with a specific institution and are more likely to enroll;
- Affiliate staff gain familiarity with the local institution(s) their TSIC students are likely to attend;
- Students gain a stronger understanding of the FAFSA application process;
- Partnerships maximize efficiency as each partner shares its expertise and possibly resources; and
- Some affiliates report financial benefits of longer-term partnerships with local post-secondary institutions, such as tuition scholarships or fee waivers designated specifically for TSIC alumni who enroll.

Challenges of Partnership

While rich benefits to partnerships prove abundant, partnerships also can be difficult to forge between nonprofits and post-secondary institutions. Primarily, the two types of entities often have vastly different organizational cultures and priorities, presenting barriers to positive communication (Barnett et al, 2012). Similarly, colleges and nonprofits may evaluate their success using different metrics as well as data systems (Conway, Blair, & Helmer, 2012). Throughout the process, it is critical to maintain ongoing communication, although limited resources can hamper the sustainability of this type of activity and relationship. One way to overcome this divide is to have a point of contact at the post-secondary institution who will spearhead the effort.

This point of contact should be re-established each school year to support an ongoing relationship despite staff turnover within the institution. However, these champions can be hard to find.

Finally, several of the affiliates interviewed noted that affiliate/post-secondary partnerships can be time-intensive to both develop and sustain, and post-secondary leadership may be hesitant about adding additional responsibilities to their staff's workload.

Affiliates aiming to enter into such partnerships should be aware that the bulk of the responsibilities related to partnership maintenance may fall on their staff. Additionally, there may be financial costs to account for, such as room rentals, travel expenses for affiliate staff, transportation for students attending campus-based events, event supplies, etc. Thus, it is critical for affiliates to ensure programmatic capacity before attempting to forge a post-secondary partnership.

Partnerships prove mutually beneficial for the organizations and especially students, but they must be implemented deliberately to be effective. This manual provides a proven framework and approach to guide TSIC affiliates in creating, fostering, and sustaining partnerships with local post-secondary institutions.

Expert Tip:

Identifying a champion at your partnering institution is a critical step toward developing a productive working relationship. Please see Attachment B for more tips on how to find and cultivate a champion.

CHAPTER (2) Research

While research about partnerships between non-profits and post-secondary institutions is limited, it points to a number of themes that can support TSIC's efforts to strengthen and codify this type of work. The following section is designed to present a landscape scan of non-profit/educational institution partnerships. For more information on affiliates who have successfully forged post-secondary partnerships, please contact the TSIC State Office.

The Aspen Institute and Workforce Strategies Initiative spearheaded the Courses to Employment (C2E) demonstration with a worthy goal: to understand how community colleges and nonprofits can effectively partner to support and spur learners on to success in post-secondary education and eventually in the workforce. In their report on the project, the authors write, "C2E is premised on the idea that by partnering, colleges and nonprofits expand their capacity and are able to leverage resources to serve more students" (Conway, Blair, & Helmer, 2012, pg. 5). Overall, upon completion, participants obtained employment and higher wages than before the training. One can classify program activities into three overarching categories: education strategies (such as individualized work plans and college entrance exam prep); support strategies (such as case management, financial assistance, and support groups); and industry strategies (such as working with employers to inform curriculum). One key research finding focused on students' needs for extra support in navigating post-secondary systems. Nonprofits can help prepare them for those systems, and colleges can

consider adjusting those systems to make them easier to learn.

A variety of studies bring these findings to light. In a case study about a career pathway for healthcare workers in Chicago, Dr. Ricardo Acarda describes "bridge programs" as those designed to "bridge the gap between the initial skills of individuals and what they need to enter and succeed in post-secondary education and career-path employment [using] three required components—contextualized instruction, career development, and support services" (Conway, Blair, & Helmer, 2012, pg. 6). Students learn generalized skills (in this case, the English language) within the context of the career path, as well as connect with potential jobs and gain non-academic support around issues that might present barriers to their career success.

Similarly, the Capital IDEA program in Austin, Texas, provides both academic and non-academic support for non-traditional students, and serves as an employment pipeline through partnerships with local colleges. They provide not only academic support, but also financial aid and childcare assistance to make college a reality for many participants.

Other research focuses on college readiness programs. Elisabeth Barnett (et al, 2012) advocates for post-secondary institutions taking an active role in facilitating the transition from high school to college. Better alignment facilitated by partnerships would lead to fewer students needing remedial coursework plus improved college readiness and outcomes in college. In a meta-analysis of college-readiness programs in Texas, Barnett and her co-authors highlighted a number of characteristics of the programs they studied:

1. Partnerships varied in intensity from coordination to collaboration.
2. Partnerships required institutional commitment, including dedicated staff and a presence in high schools.
3. Successful partnerships had a champion with a deep interest in the program.
4. Funding and policy mandates influenced the intensity and focus of the programs.

College Success Arizona demonstrates many of these factors. The program supports graduating high school seniors with scholarships and mentoring throughout college.

This includes mentoring and support around a range of topics including financial aid, transitioning from community college to a four-year university, and freshman retention. Success Advisors provide this mentoring to almost all applicants to the program, regardless of whether they are awarded a scholarship (https://collegesuccessarizona.org/).

Two themes tend to run throughout all the research about partnerships between nonprofits and post-secondary institutions:

- The need for a memorandum of understanding, outlining responsibilities, and
- Opportunities for data-sharing.

These themes are documented by the Annenberg Institute for School Reform at Brown University (2013), which used a partnership between San Jose Unified School District and the University of California, Berkeley, as an example. Here, the district share students' transcripts to be evaluated based on the university's benchmarks. This allows UC Berkeley to support their guidance counselor fellowship program, and participating schools can better prepare their students for college.

In conjunction with Take Stock in Children's experiences, these analyses and examples can inform a new structure for partnerships with post-secondary institutions.

CHAPTER (3) TSIC Post-Secondary Partnership Model

Communication	• Ongoing communication between TSIC and post-secondary staff is critical to success. (**See Attachment A for a suggested meeting agenda.**)
Events	• Events often take place on college campuses and are facilitated by college staff. • Topics include (but are not limited to) tours, academic and financial aid workshops, and career panels.
Setting Expectations	• Being clear on roles at the partnership's outset proves critical. • A signed Memorandum of Understanding helps ensure longevity, even with staff turnover. (See Attachment C, E, and F for tips.)
Data Sharing	• Define clear metrics and decide on reporting accountability. • Students must agree to data sharing and be assured their privacy will be protected. (See Attachment D's checklist to prepare for effective data sharing.)
Champion	• Having a relationship with a "champion" leader from the post-secondary institution to spearhead and advocate for the partnership is central to sustaining success. (See Attachment B for relationship-building ideas.)
Staffing	• Building and maintaining partnerships requires staffing resources; this can be maximized by staff who are accountable to both organizations.

Overview of TSIC Post-Secondary Partnerships

Many Take Stock in Children affiliates partner with local post-secondary institutions, primarily community colleges. To understand current activities to pursue post-secondary partnerships, interviews were completed with eight TSIC affiliates. Questions focused on qualities of the relationship, benefits and challenges of partnership, readiness factors, expectations, and data sharing. While each partnership was different, certain components emerged that echo the research base.

These elements are directly connected to the benefits TSIC affiliates identified. Primarily, students gain familiarity with the post-secondary environment and extra support around financial aid and navigating their next steps. These partnerships extend the deep impact of TSIC's mentoring and college success coach model to best equip students for post-secondary education.

Steps to Build a Post-Secondary Education Partnership

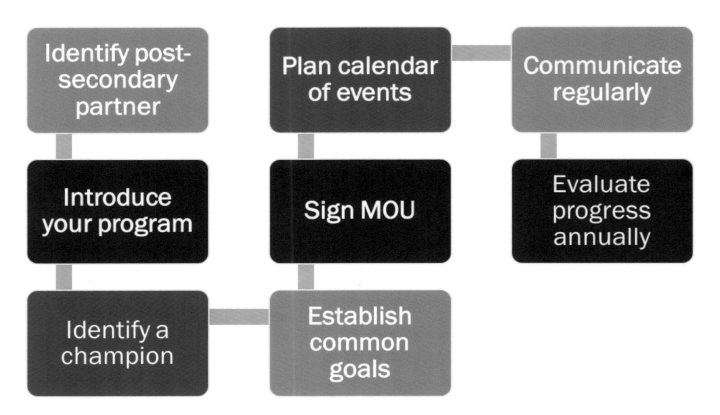

A strong partnership is based on a solid foundation with clear expectations and can be created through a series of steps with regular opportunities for evaluation and refinement.

Affiliates noted that the process of developing a post-secondary partnership often happened slowly, over a year or more. There is no set timeline over which these steps should occur; it is fine (and even advisable!) to move slowly and allow trust and familiarity to build between the two parties. This will ensure deliberate and thoughtful action at each step and result in a better chance of achieving success.

Step 1: Identify Post-Secondary Education Partner(s)

Consider the post-secondary education institutions in the region. At the outset of creating a partnership, look for conditions for success:

- Which institutions have high matriculation rates from TSIC participating high schools?
- Which are local and seem under-utilized, with opportunities for growth?
- Which ones have robust student preparation programs and/or are active in the community?

A TSIC affiliate might have more than one post-secondary partner where multiple positive opportunities exist.

Expert Tip:

When choosing a partnering institution, consider whether your affiliate staff have pre-existing relationships with staff at a local campus or are alumni themselves. These connections could help you achieve Step 2 (Introduce Your Program).

Step 2: Introduce Your Program to Institution Leadership

Affiliates that have successfully forged post-secondary partnerships noted the criticality of garnering recognition (and ultimately, approval) from the top. If you are not already connected to your identified institution's leadership, your next step should be introducing yourself to the college/university president

or program director. Start by asking for a brief introductory meeting, with a goal of familiarizing their administration with TSIC's mission and model. See the bulleted list below for talking point suggestions.

If you find it difficult to gain introduction to an institution's president or director, it may be helpful to contact the State Office, who may be able to assist with setting an introductory meeting.

Once a meeting is scheduled, develop an agenda that includes the following:

- An introduction to the TSIC network and a brief summary of your affiliate's work
- A synopsis of your affiliate's history with the institution (how many TSIC students are currently in attendance, have graduated, etc.)
- Case study examples of TSIC alumni who have successfully graduated from their program, if applicable
- Time for them to share their own institutional goals and how they see TSIC contributing
- Time to discuss who else on campus/ which offices or departments might be interested in learning more about TSIC

This meeting's goal should primarily focus on building familiarity and opening the door for further communications. However, it may be appropriate to request a small "ask," such as permission to recruit for mentors on campus, etc.

When writing a letter of introduction to the institution president or program director, consider these "Dos and Don'ts":

- Do include a brief summary of TSIC; do highlight statistics on TSIC/your affiliate's success and the number of TSIC alumni who have graduated/are currently enrolled in their program; and do politely ask for a meeting to introduce yourself and provide more information on how the TSIC model benefits their current and future students.
- Don't ask for anything beyond an introductory meeting; and don't forget to include how your program is poised to provide benefits to the institution via a working relationship – such as providing more student applicants.

Step 3: Identify a Champion

Finding a program champion, ideally someone with decision-making authority, is critical to building a strong base. Over time, this champion may also be interested in becoming a member of a local TSIC Leadership Council, effectively furthering the commitment to collaborate with TSIC. See Attachment B for tips on cultivating these relationships.

Step 4: Establish Common Goals

Stakeholders should establish a shared understanding of the nature of the partnership and objectives of working together to help middle and high school students become college ready. This addresses the challenge of disparate cultures and goals that is common to this type of partnership. See Attachment C for a meeting agenda structured to define these common goals.

Expert Tip: As mentioned above, it may be advisable to set small goals in the beginning and then expand the scope as the partnership develops. For example, one affiliate started with holding a joint FAFSA completion workshop with its partnering institution and ensured this event was successful before adopting bigger goals.

Step 5: Sign MOU

The partnership goals, infrastructure, roles, and responsibilities should be codified in a memorandum of understanding (MOU) signed by both partners. This document should be re-visited and edited at least annually. See Attachments E and F for guidelines and a sample MOU.

Be diligent to ensure any agreed-upon responsibilities are put into writing, even when all parties are clearly in agreement. This will help ensure that the partnership stays in place, even if staff or leadership turnover occurs at the partnering institution.

Step 6: Plan Calendar of Events

The MOU should facilitate the planning and implementation of a series of events designed to prepare students for applying to and matriculating in a post-secondary institution. These events align with partnership goals and may include activities such as FAFSA workshops, campus tours, and coaching sessions.

Step 7: Communicate Regularly

Ongoing communication among stakeholders creates a sustainable partnership that evolves with students' needs and responds to successes and challenges. Strategies for communication should be incorporated into the MOU and include group meetings and one-on-one check-ins between each organization's point person. Communication should include a formal annual review of the MOU. Concurrent to formal meetings, informal, frequent communications can be just as crucial as formal communication vehicles, especially when a challenge arises. Depending on the type of relationship, you may want to check in monthly or quarterly, even if only briefly, to ensure the partnership is functioning well and to everyone's benefit.

Expert Tip:

In addition to regular communication, it is important to continue building your partnering institution's awareness of TSIC's impact. Be sure to invite institutional leadership and any staff/faculty who have contributed to the partnership to attend your affiliate's celebratory events such as holiday parties and graduation.

Step 8: Evaluate Progress

As with any new initiative, it is always advisable to regularly evaluate your progress. At the end of the partnership's first year, schedule a meeting with relevant affiliate staff and representation from the partnering institution to review the process thus far, reflect on any needed changes from either party, and plan for next steps.

Partnership Continuum

Partnerships fall along a continuum from coordination to collaboration (Barnett, et al., 2012). Affiliates can consider where they currently fall on the path and what areas present potential for expansion.

Currently, affiliate types fall into four main categories:

1) Stand-alone nonprofits with Take Stock in Children as the sole program;

2) Education or public school foundations that implement a number of programs, including Take Stock in Children;

3) Colleges or college foundations that implement Take Stock in Children, among other programs; and

4) Public school systems that implement Take Stock in Children as a student service.

Partnership Staffing

Staff support for post-secondary partnerships will vary based on affiliate model. When a college foundation is the lead agency for TSIC, staff is likely embedded into the foundation and inherently accountable to both the foundation and TSIC affiliate. A stand-alone affiliate will have contacts at a college (or many colleges) who have no formal responsibility to TSIC. One way to progress toward collaboration is to incorporate TSIC/post-secondary elements into job descriptions. Some suggested job responsibilities (which can be edited or pasted directly into a job description) include the following:

- ✓ Attend/facilitate regular meetings between TSIC and post-secondary institution to assess partnership status and coordinate future endeavors (both)

- ✓ Communicate directly with TSIC/post-secondary point person to coordinate specific events (both)

- ✓ Identify key people on campus to engage as TSIC advocates (TSIC)

- ✓ Ensure that at least 25% of student activities are coordinated with the post-secondary institution (TSIC)

- ✓ Serve as point person for TSIC program on campus (post-secondary)

- ✓ Fundraise for TSIC to be implemented on campus (post-secondary)

A limited number of affiliates are incorporated into another nonprofit (such as Goodwill Industries, Big Brothers Big Sisters, or the YMCA).

These contexts may impact the ways that TSIC affiliates and post-secondary institutions build relationships. Affiliates that are part of a college or college foundation have an agreement embedded in the model and generally share staff. Those that have no exchanging relationship with a post-secondary institution may visit campus for events but do not have back-and-forth collaboration. These two ends of the continuum are approaching post-secondary institutional partnerships from different starting places and, accordingly, will often take different action steps to advance their efforts to serve students and prepare them for post-secondary education.

Partnership Rubric

Based on the current state, affiliates should consider six areas and determine appropriate steps to move from coordination to collaboration. The ultimate goal of the progression presented in this rubric is for local affiliates and post-secondary institutions to effectively work together to contribute to the college readiness of students in middle and high school. Refer to the attachments for supporting documents for further details. To be connected with affiliates currently maintaining partnerships along this continuum, please contact the TSIC State Office.

Partnership Element	Coordination				Collaboration
Level	1	2	3	4	5
Communication	Communication is informal and irregular.	Include communication with post-secondary staff as part of TSIC job description.	Convene annual kick-off meeting to discuss shared activities.	Convene quarterly meetings.	Designated staff from TSIC and post-secondary institution meet on a regular basis (at least monthly) to discuss partnership.
Champion/ Relationships	Informal relationships with staff without decision-making authority	Build awareness of the partnership among college leadership	Include partnership responsibilities in post-secondary job descriptions	Post-secondary leadership attends regular TSIC meetings.	Post-secondary champion at administrative/leader-ship level spear-heads partnership.
Setting Expectations	Little or no conversation about goals and structure of partnership.	Discuss goals and responsibilities for each specific event and otherwise as needed	Define responsibilities that encompass all annual events.	Discuss roles and partnership objectives in a structured setting.	Sign an MOU based on group brainstorm, which includes roles, responsibilities, and project objectives.
Events	• Events are planned ad hoc. • May take place at college or high school. • General topics for all students. • College tours	• Set an annual schedule at the beginning of the academic year. • Workshops held at high schools or post-secondary institutions but facilitated by TSIC staff	• Include opportunities for students to visit campus and see campus representatives at their high school.	• Workshops held in both places, facilitated by post-secondary staff. • Workshops go beyond financial aid and focus on other skills to help students become college-ready.	Align events with academic and non academic goals Include opportunities for tailored support for students (e.g., financial aid application support, course registration). non-academic goals.
Data Sharing	No outcomes are measured.	Partners maintain their own metrics and data systems	Partners share data upon request. Accounts for student privacy.	Partners discuss metrics that align with project goals and have tools to measure these outcomes. Accounts for student privacy.	Both partners are accountable for sharing data with the other and use compatible data systems. Included in MOU. Accounts for student privacy.
Staffing	No dedicated staffing for partnership, particularly from university/college.	TSIC staff job description includes responsibility for managing post-secondary relationships/ activities	Both TSIC and post-secondary institution have staff who have TSIC as a core responsibility.	TSIC staff members are embedded at the post-secondary institution.	Staff assigned as a primary point of contact and accountable to both organizations.

Activity: Using the Partnership Rubric and Defining Action Steps

1) Using the rubric above, identify where your affiliate falls from 1-5 in each of the six core elements. You may find that you are in a different place for each element—and that's okay!

2) For each element, identify 1-3 concrete action steps you will take this year to move toward the next level. You might prioritize some elements rather than try to do everything at once.

Example: Moving from Communication Level 2 to Level 3

Affiliate has a staff person responsible for communication with the local college, but this communication happens infrequently and with a variety of people.

Action Steps:

1) Convene a kick-off meeting in the summer to talk about TSIC's plans for the coming year and how the college can be involved.

   a. Invite all people who have already participated and ask them if any others should be involved.
   b. Include a student to tell his or her story.
   c. Ask advice on how to strengthen the partnership.
2) After meeting, develop email group of all attendees and send regular updates.

Maintaining Communication

Regardless of where a partnership falls in the rubric, it is vital for the TSIC affiliate to maintain frequent communication with its post-secondary partner. Depending on the topic, these interactions should happen with varying frequency:

Monthly (or weekly if needed): Check-ins will largely revolve around logistics for events. What needs to be done, and who is responsible?

Bi-annually (midyear/end-of-year): Evaluate the successes of the first half of the year and make appropriate adjustments to second semester. Review data and progress toward goals and confirm plans for evaluation.

Annually (beginning of year): Review the MOU and make changes based on prior year. Confirm points of contact and revisit the rubric together, considering what action steps the partners might take to progress to the next level in one or more areas.

Consistent communication is the key to strengthening and growing the partnership. It will ensure that all parties involved are kept informed on a regular basis of the progress and impact of the partnership.

CHAPTER 4 **Frequently Asked Questions (FAQs**

Q: We have a small TSIC staff team, and we all have a lot to do. How do I make time for this kind of partnership?

A: Creating and maintaining partnerships with post-secondary institutions can take time and effort. Prioritize those elements of the partnership that may make the process more efficient and save time in the long run, as well as have the most impact on students. For example, it may take time to build a relationship with a college's financial aid office, but if their staff can eventually facilitate and host FAFSA workshops, this time up-front will likely be worthwhile. Also, summer can be a great time to begin a partnership process. Starting small with a joint event or workshop can initiate a relationship that can then continue to grow.

Q: Try as I might, I can't get traction with a partner champion. How should I proceed?

A: First, consider whether there is someone else at the institution who might be a better fit. For example, if you are trying to engage the president, perhaps the dean of the school of education would be more likely to take interest. Or the president's office may be able to steer you to the appropriate office where a champion would best serve TSIC. Often the Vice President or Director of Student Services is a great resource since they often oversee dual enrollment programs, student recruitment, and admissions. Second, analyze other individuals who might be close to your potential champion. The president's executive assistant might have influence on his/her schedule and priorities. Once you have exhausted options, it is worth assessing whether this partner holds potential for growth. If not, you may decide not to invest as many resources in activities with this partner and instead focus attention on a different partner.

Q: How long will it take to create a partnership like this?

A: This depends largely on the context. It will take at least a year to establish a working partnership and then additional time to move up the levels of the rubric, depending on the commitment of both partners. To begin, the affiliate should research how many high school graduates matriculate annually into their institution. Once the partners realize success with events, workshops, or other activities, the partners recognize the impact and will be motivated to continue and grow the partnership.

Q: How often should we meet?

A: Meeting frequency will vary based on the partnership's nature and position in the rubric. See Chapter 3 for some guidelines on when to communicate about which topics.

ATTACHMENT A

Implementation Tools – Sample Regular Meeting Agenda

The following agenda could be used for any regular meeting with TSIC and post-secondary staff to discuss the partnership. It should be tailored based on the meeting frequency.

Sample Meeting Agenda

1. Introductions (include reminder of staff responsibilities relating to TSIC)
2. Review of previous events since last meeting
   a. Number of students attended
   b. Specific metrics of success (e.g., X students submitted their FAFSA forms)
   c. Feedback and ideas for next time
3. Upcoming events
   a. Clarification of roles and responsibilities
   b. Review of goals
   c. To-dos
4. New ideas for future events
   a. Ensure they fit with goals and expectations
5. Data review
   a. Progress toward goals
   a. Application/enrollment update – student status
6. Other news and updates

ATTACHMENT B:

Implementation Tools – Tips for Finding a Champion

The ideal program champion will have the winning combination of authority, enthusiasm, and expertise. It may be advisable to assemble a team of people representing these qualities. Here are some characteristics to look for when assessing potential candidates:

Authority: Can this person influence or make decisions on behalf of the post-secondary institution?

- Head of a department
- Committee lead
- Works closely with institution leadership

Enthusiasm: Is this person excited about TSIC and its mission?

- Understanding of program goals
- Attended past TSIC events or graduation

Expertise: Is this person equipped to contribute to the team's ideas and activities?

- Department is aligned with TSIC goals (e.g., campus tours, admissions, student life, financial aid, academic support)
- Experience working with TSIC students or similar demographic

Building relationships with those who embody these characteristics may take time. Suggestions for fostering these connections include the following:

- ✓ Distribute promotional TSIC materials to key departments and follow up with phone calls/ emails to answer questions. Be sure to include key metrics about how a partnership will benefit them (e.g., increased enrollment, better prepared students, etc.).
- ✓ Host an annual breakfast or lunch event; invite key institution staff as well as current and alumni TSIC students to tell their stories; observe which guests seem most engaged, and follow up.
- ✓ Build connections with those who are close with institutional leadership, such as administrative assistants; work to engage them so they will encourage their bosses to get involved.
- ✓ Recruit volunteer mentors from the campus staff.
- ✓ Invite campus leaders to TSIC events (workshops, tours, graduation, etc.).

✓ Consider forging relationships with leaders at the education department on campus; they are likely to have a strong academic interest in TSIC and may be helpful allies.

✓ Always stress that the partnership is mutually beneficial. A partnership could greatly benefit the post-secondary institution by increasing student applications and better preparing enrolled students to be successful.

ATTACHMENT C

Implementation Tools – Setting Goals and Expectations

One key success factor is making sure everyone from TSIC and post-secondary partners have common goals and expectations. Once you have configured a team who will be involved in the partnership, designate time as a group to distill your core objectives and a structure for achieving them. A sample activity agenda follows (this might be split across multiple meetings):

1) Define goals:

    a. As a group, brainstorm all goals for the partnership on chart paper or white board. Together, answer the question, Why are we working together? Be clear that this is designed as mutually beneficial. Some examples include the following:

        1. Assist TSIC students with financial aid applications

        2. Increase enrollment at the post-secondary institution

        3. Give TSIC students the opportunity to interact with current post-secondary students

    b. Give each participant 3–5 stickers (foil stars or colored dots work well). Choose the number based on how many participants you have and how many goals you want to identify.

    c. Ask each participant to place their stickers next to their top choices for goals to focus on through the TSIC-College Partnership. Remind the group that this is your first set of goals and you may return to this list to identify other priorities in the future.

    d. Tally the stickers — the goals with the most stickers become your focus.

    e. If there are no obvious "winners," do two rounds. After the first round, give just 5–7 choices and vote again.

2) Clarify responsibilities:

    a. Write each goal at the top of a piece of chart paper (one page for each goal).

    b. Beneath the goal, write "What," "TSIC," and the post-secondary name.

    c. Either in the large group or in pairs, decide what activities will be related to the goal and what each party's responsibilities are for facilitating these activities. See the figure on the next page for a sample.

    d. If in groups, report back. Ensure everyone is comfortable with these decisions.

3) Define and list inputs:

    a. For success in these efforts, certain infrastructure inputs need to be in place. Consider these the "rules of engagement." What does everyone need to commit to doing in order to create a strong foundation for other activities? List these together, and be as specific as you'd like. Examples include the following:

1. Meet as a group every month
2. Respond to emails/calls within 48 hours
3. Designate a point person from each organization (list names)
4. Include both logos on collateral materials

Note: These discussions and decisions will vary in robustness based on the stage of the partnership. No matter where your group falls on the spectrum, from coordination to collaboration, this still offers a worthwhile exercise. The information should be included in your signed MOU. (See Attachment E for details).

Sample Chart Paper

Goal: Students will complete FAFSA applications

What: FAFSA workshop

TSIC: Bring students to workshop; follow up to ensure submission

ATTACHMENT D:

Implementation Tools – Tips for Building Efficient and Effective Data Systems

Do your metrics meet these criteria? Are they . . .

ALIGNED?

- They are directly related to partnership goals.
- They have specific targets based on historical data.

DO:

- ✓ List desired outcomes as part of goal-setting activity. For example, if your goal is to increase TSIC student applications to a college from a specific county, a metric could be, "Increase TSIC student applications from that county by 5%."

DON'T:

- ✗ Identify outcomes in a vacuum. If your goal is to increase applications from a specific high school, the metric should not be, "Increase enrollment from high school by 5%.

MEASURABLE?

- Specific tools are in place that measure desired outcome.
- Tool is accessible and realistic to use.

DO:

- ✓ Rely on information already collected or that can be integrated into an existing process. For example, count applications received, or add a simple question to an existing form that is already collected.

DON'T:

- ✗ Implement tedious measures that will be difficult to collect. For example, a paper survey that takes 30 minutes for a graduating high school senior to fill out over the summer will likely have a low response rate.

EFFICIENT?

- Data is shared between partners along a specified schedule.

- Partners both have access to the same system.
- Students are aware of and permit data collection and analysis.

DO:

- ✓ Incorporate data sharing and grants into your MOU.

- ✓ Gain a strong understanding of what your partner already collects, how, and who is responsible for it.

- ✓ Have students sign permission for data collection that extends through their college years and can follow them to a different institution.

DON'T:

- ✗ Surprise your partner with data requests and be compliant with FERPA regulations.

- ✗ Collect the same information as your partner, separately.

- ✗ Rely on student permission that must be re-collected every year.

ATTACHMENT E

Implementation Tools – How to Create an MOU

Please note: This section is not intended as legal advice. It is always advised to consult with legal counsel when entering into a new contract.

A Memorandum of Understanding (MOU) is designed to outline expectations. Regardless of the level of collaboration, it is important to outline the roles that each party will play in building a partnership between TSIC and the post-secondary institution. The MOU can serve as an important tool to guide future meetings, check-in on progress, and make adjustments based on past learning. Use the information compiled by using this guide and the other appendices, and make sure to include the following:

1. Partnership objectives
   a. What goals is this MOU designed to facilitate?
   b. Why are TSIC and the post-secondary institution working together?
   c. Is the partnership designed to familiarize students with post-secondary campuses in general? Help them complete financial aid applications? Prepare them for non-academic tasks in college?

2. Communication
   a. Who are the point people from each organization?
   b. How often will the point people meet?

3. Program structure
   a. What goals will structured activities accomplish?
   b. What are the general responsibilities of each party when planning activities?

4. Evaluation
   a. What metrics will be measured?
   b. What tools will be used to measure these metrics?
   c. What data will be shared? How often?
   d. Who will you analyze the data?

5. Funding
   a. Are there financial requirements from either side? Make sure to include these commitments.

6. Ending the partnership
   a. Are there any reasons the partnership might end? What are they?
   b. What is the process to discontinue the partnership?

See also the sample MOU, Attachment F.

ATTACHMENT F:

Sample MOU

Sample Memorandum of Understanding (MOU) for TSIC and Post-Secondary Partners

It is considered a best practice for a Take Stock in Children affiliate and its post-secondary partners to sign a Memorandum of Understanding (MOU). An MOU outlines roles, responsibilities, and expectations, and helps strengthen partnerships.

The following is a sample MOU that illustrates the areas that partners might wish to include in their agreement. Affiliates should edit this to be appropriate for their unique situations.

This Memorandum of Understanding (MOU) is entered into by and between the following entities: _____ and _____

These entities are partnering to support students enrolled in the Take Stock in Children (TSIC) intervention. TSIC provides a unique opportunity for deserving low-income youth/students to escape the cycle of poverty through education. The program offers students post-secondary scholarships, caring volunteer mentors, and hope for a better life. The comprehensive services start in middle school, continue through high school, and include their transition into post-secondary education.

I.   Scope of Work
Each group applicant agrees to participate in the proposed partnership and work collaboratively toward the shared goals. These goals include the following:

Insert goals and objectives as determined during group discussion

II.   Joint Responsibilities for Communications and Development of Timelines
Each group understands that ongoing and consistent communication is necessary for a strong partnership in service of students' success.

1.   Each group member will appoint a key contact person for the grant.
2.   These key contacts will maintain frequent communication to facilitate cooperation under this MOU.
3.   These key contacts will work together to determine needs and to provide project updates and status reports.

The point person/people for _____ are: _____

The point person/people for _____ are: _____

Regular communication will take place via insert frequency and type of meetings.

III. Responsibilities

A number of events and activities will structure the partnership. Both partners will play important roles in making sure these are a success and help advance the mission. Each party agrees to the following responsibilities:

TSIC will be responsible for the following: insert responsibilities

Partner will be responsible for the following: insert responsibilities

IV. Evaluation and Data Sharing

The partners have agreed to the following metrics to assess progress toward goals:

Insert agreed upon metrics

To measure these outcomes, each partner will agree to collect and share the following information:

TSIC will insert data sharing responsibilities

Partner will insert data sharing responsibilities

V. Fiscal Responsibility

Insert any information regarding fiscal responsibility (i.e., grants, payments, etc.)

VI. Working Relationship Among Group Members

The following guidelines will be followed to ensure partners uphold their responsibilities:

To be filled in according to the agreement of the members and the design of the project. This section might address the members' agreement on the steps to be taken in the event one member is not fulfilling its responsibilities.

VII. Modifications

This MOU may be amended only by written agreement signed by each group member. A formal review of the MOU will occur annually, at which point partners will assess successes and challenges and set priorities for the coming year.

VIII. Effective Date/Duration/Termination

This MOU shall be effective beginning with the date of the last signature hereon. It will be reviewed each year and modifications can be made at that time. In the event that one partner wants to discontinue the partnership, they will request a meeting with the other partner for information sharing. The ending of the partnership will be put into writing, with each party agreeing to fulfill any final responsibilities that work in service of the students.

Insert any pre-defined reasons for ending partnership

XII. Signatures

   3) TSIC Affiliate

   _____

   Signature/Date

   _____

   Print Name/Title/Name of Affiliate

   _____

   4) Post-Secondary Education Partner Representative

   _____

   Signature/Date

   _____

   Print Name/Title/Name of Institution

   _____

ATTACHMENT G:

References

Annenberg Institute for Education Reform. (2013). *Partnerships for College Readiness*. Brown University. Retrieved from http://www.annenberginstitute.org/sites/default/files/PartnershipReport.pdf

Arcada, R. *How to Build Bridge Programs That Fit into a Career Pathway: A Step-by-Step Guide Based on the Carreras en Salud Program in Chicago*. Retrieved from http://www.idpl.org/images/publicationsPDFs/Instituto2010_HowToBuildBridgePrograms%20final.pdf

Barnett, Elisabeth, et al. (2012) *Preparing High School Students for College: An Exploratory Study of College Readiness Partnership Programs in Texas*. Retrieved from https://doi.org/10.7916/D80R9MF9

College Success Arizona. https://collegesuccessarizona.org/

Conway, C., Blair, A., and Helmer, M. (2012) *Courses to Employment: Partnering to Create Paths to Education and Careers*. Aspen Institute, Washington, DC.

Take Stock Innovation Collection: Group Mentoring

Take Stock in
Children®

The contents of this manual were developed under a grant from the
U.S. Department of Education, Investing in Innovation (i3) Program.
However, those contents do not necessarily represent the policy of
the U.S. Department of Education, and you should not assume
endorsement by the federal government.

Table of Contents

ACKNOWLEDGEMENTS

Take Stock in Children (TSIC) would like to thank and acknowledge the UNISON team that has tirelessly worked to launch and successfully implement the innovations supported by TSIC's Investing in Innovation (i3) grant. This team, led by Judy Saylor, Director of Program Growth and Innovation, includes Tiara Arline, Sara Buckley, Tiffany Givens, Amy Grunder, Roxanne Jordan, and Luz Rodriguez. The i3 grant program is ultimately about reaching scale—taking innovations from pilot to multiple sites and programs. Through the hard work of this team, innovations will impact over 8,500 per year through 45 independent affiliates across the TSIC network.

TSIC would also like to give a special thanks to the Take Stock in Children local affiliates who contributed their time and expertise to field test and refine the group mentoring model. These affiliates include: Take Stock in Children Jacksonville; the Foundation for Florida Gateway College (serving Baker, Columbia, Dixie, Gilchrist, and Union counties); the Hillsborough Education Foundation; The Immokalee Foundation; Take Stock in Children Palm Beach; and the Pinellas Education Foundation.

Finally, TSIC would like to recognize Gary Romano and the Civitas Strategies team for guiding the codification and scaling process of the innovations developed during the i3 grant program.

The increased number of students served and continually growing demand mean that UNISON innovations will provide the network with opportunities that efficiently use resources and maintain a high level of programmatic quality and service delivery. Scaling these elements will not only benefit the TSIC network but will also accelerate the progress of national scaling efforts. Network-wide adoption will effectively result in additional proof points and data, contributing to a climate conducive to national uptake.

Introduction

The Take Stock in Children (TSIC) model of support is built upon the positive relationships that students develop with their mentors. The impact that a caring adult can have on a student's academic and social-emotional development has been proven in field-based research. There is strong evidence that a community-based mentoring approach decreases drug and alcohol use, enhances peer and parent-child relationships, increases school attendance, and improves attitudes about and performance in school (Tierney, Grossman and Resch, 1995). These positive results are also illustrated in the outstanding results of TSIC students. Each TSIC child is matched with a caring adult mentor who meets with the student at his/her school for an hour each week. Mentors provide academic and behavioral motivation, guidance, friendship, and support.

The overall success of the program along with the increasing number of students in need has encouraged affiliates to target growth in an effort to increase the number of students served across the organization.

Group mentoring is an approach that can help organizations continue to effectively and efficiently support greater numbers of students.

Effective mentor support has greatly contributed to TSIC's results with:

96% of Take Stock in Children students graduate high school on time

92% of Take Stock in Children students enter post-secondary education

68% of The Stock in Children Students complete post-secondary education, compared to the state average of 27% for at-risk students in poverty

However, this growth also presents challenges, especially with regard to finding the number of mentors needed to serve the increasing population of students. This is especially true for rural programs. Therefore, TSIC is looking to alternative forms of mentoring that preserve quality but are also more efficient. TSIC is looking to promote higher rates of mentor matching in order to ultimately serve even more students in need.

In this hybrid-mentoring model, groups of students meet with a mentor on a regular basis. Utilizing this type of model is not exclusive to mentoring programs.

Different fields, including clinical and school psychology, education, and social work, all frequently use group interventions for both children and adolescents. "Meta-analyses have concluded that group therapies, particularly those employing cognitive-behavioral techniques, are effective for treating substance abuse, aggression, and anxiety disorders among youth. In some analyses, the effects of group therapies are comparable, if not superior, to those of individual therapies" (Kuperminc, 2016).

The TSIC group mentoring model is a strategy that was developed through TSIC's UNISON project, a federally funded Investing in Innovation (i3) grant implemented at three school sites where group mentoring was the preferred model. The lessons learned from this project were instrumental in codifying the model for replication across the network.

This group-mentoring manual is the result of that codification and will present information needed for launching and implementing the TSIC Group Mentoring Model.

Material covered in this manual includes:

- The definition of group mentoring;
- When to use group mentoring;
- The benefits of group mentoring;
- The challenges of group mentoring and how to address them;
- Strategies for group mentors including first contact and meetings; and
- Tools for group mentoring implementation.

Launching any new program can be challenging, regardless of the depth of instructions. If you have any questions not covered in the manual or feedback in general you would like to share, please contact the TSIC State Office or your Regional Director.

CHAPTER (1) Why Group Mentoring? Definition

Group mentoring offers students and mentors experiences that are just as similar and as mutually beneficial as the traditional TSIC 1:1 mentoring model. This group-oriented experience empowers students to become advocates for their success by sharing information and offering advice, social support, coaching, and counseling.

Characteristics of Group Mentoring

✓ At least two students

✓ One volunteer mentor

✓ Groups meet at least 2x per month for 30 minutes

✓ Meetings held at commonly convenient times (e.g., during lunch time or after school) and locations (e.g., media center, guidance conference room)

✓ Occurs at a TSIC-sanctioned location such as a school

✓ Should be used by no more than 10% of an affiliate's students

✓ Group mentoring implementation plan must be submitted by programs and approved by the State Office

Benefits of Group Mentoring

There are a number of benefits that have been reported by sites that have piloted the group mentoring approach.

Fewer Mentors Needed — It can often be challenging for small TSIC programs or those located in rural settings to find high numbers of volunteers to deliver 1:1 mentoring. This, in turn, is a rate-limiting factor on program growth. Effective use of the group mentoring approach has the potential to ease the number of mentors required to meet TSIC standards and offer quality services.

Richer Discussions — Staff, mentors, and students alike report that another benefit of the group mentoring setting is that deep discussions are easier to establish when several well-matched students are together in a room. Students and mentors tend to be more comfortable and relaxed because they don't feel pressure to talk.

Peer-to-Peer Support — Group mentoring not only offers mentor-student support but also offers a support system of fellow students helping one another. Students in group mentoring settings know they have a caring adult in their lives, but they also know that they have their peers on campus every day whom they can turn to versus having to wait for another session with their adult mentor.

Staff who oversee group mentoring programming also report that students are motivated to move to the next level of achievement through peer influence and support.

Challenges of Group Mentoring

While group mentoring does have clear benefits, especially for small or rural programs, it is not the best option for every student or affiliate.

For example, there may be students that either cannot be or should not be paired together. Or, some students prefer the 1:1 setting to really connect with a mentor. If a program is able, a choice should be offered to students to determine participation within a group or 1:1 mentoring.

Securing a regular meeting space that can accommodate groups can also be a challenge. To alleviate this pressure on space, it is helpful to try and spread out group meetings as much as possible. If several mentor groups meet on the same day in the same location, it can be very difficult to find space for all of them. Staff report success with asking mentors to select a consistent day/time to meet with students. They also give mentors information about which days are busy and try to fill in the gaps. Most importantly, staff should work with schools to identify creative solutions to space issues. For example, one school was willing to dedicate time during a weekly 50-minute homeroom session to group mentoring.

Additionally, afterschool settings can be a challenge because of students missing sessions. This can be frustrating for mentors who may have to travel distances to attend the session, especially when groups are small.

CHAPTER (2) Launching Group Mentoring

Overview

For any organization interested in establishing a successful group mentoring model, six specific steps should be taken to ensure model fidelity and best practice. These steps are included in the figure below and explained in greater detail throughout this section.

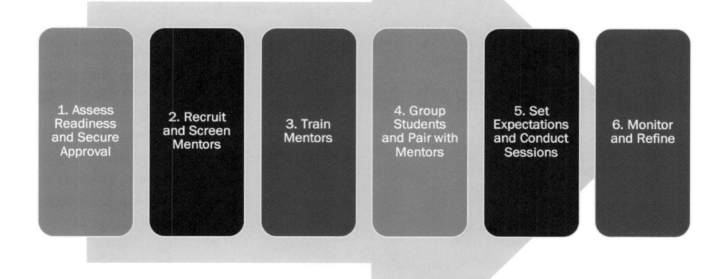

1. Assess Readiness and Secure Approval

2. Recruit and Screen Mentors

3. Train Mentors

4. Group Students and Pair with Mentors

5. Set Expectations and Conduct Sessions

6. Monitor and Refine

PART 1: ASSESS READINESS AND SECURE APPROVAL

While group mentoring is an effective way to serve more students without compromising service quality, there are specific factors that a program should have prior to implementing the model.

First, given that there are a range of logistical challenges associated with setting up group mentoring, implementing this approach is most effective in schools where a strong relationship exists between the school and TSIC, characterized by regular communication and a strong liaison or advocate. For example, having an embedded staff member, active school liaison, or a more intense and regular presence of TSIC staff members in the school offer situations that are particularly conducive to group mentoring.

Second, you want to ensure that developing clusters of students for efficient delivery is possible in your program's context. That is, you need to identify schools where it is possible to have groups of students with similar schedules so that group meetings are possible either during lunch or after school. Some schools have certain common free periods that can be used to convene groups. For example, one school has 8:00-9:00 a.m. as a free period every Monday for homework, clubs, and other activities. This would be a good choice for group mentoring. This is also a good time to investigate space and meeting place options.

Securing meeting spaces that are available and appropriate for group mentoring has proven a challenge but essential for success. It is important to address this issue early in the readiness assessment, rather than further into the student/mentor grouping process. Group mentoring requires a private space that is large enough to accommodate 4-5 students and an adult. Ideally, it should be a space where the group can face one another in a circle or be seated around a table. Also, it is important to consider whether or not multiple groups will be taking place simultaneously and secure a space that can accommodate this. If possible, obtain the class schedules for the school at the start of the academic year. This can help identify times that will be best for group mentoring to take place.

Keep in mind that the school's space commitments will change during state testing. A number of sites have reported that breakout spaces being used for group mentoring were taken up during state testing to store materials or for testing students in small groups. It is important to work out an alternate arrangement during the assessment phase.

Similarly, you want to make sure that program staff is able to effectively select students for groups based on their individual characteristics. This means that staff members need to have an understanding of who the students are and anticipate how they will work with one another and a particular mentor. This understanding should either be based on already established knowledge of the students or interactions with teachers and/or school faculty who know the students. Once again, this underscores the importance of implementing group mentoring in schools where a strong TSIC champion, advocate, or school liaison is present to support regular communication with the school.

This can help prevent phone and email "tag" that can often happen between the TSIC office and the school.

Group mentoring presents mentors with the additional challenges of managing a group of students in order to achieve impact. Because of this, it is important that group mentors have experience working with youth in educational or other extracurricular settings. Also, programs should be prepared to offer additional training to group mentors to support them as they facilitate and manage student groups.

Securing Approval — Group mentoring is a supplement to individual mentoring and should not be applied, even if a site deems itself ready per this process until they have proposed an implementation plan and been approved by the State Office. This implementation plan should be submitted to the State Office by the third business day in June each year. Even with approval, no more than 10% of an affiliate's mentors in a given school year can use group mentoring. To the right are TSIC's requirements for a group mentoring implementation plan. You can find the implementation plan form in Attachment A of this manual.

Keep in mind that the implementation plan needs to be updated and submitted for each year (by the third business day in June). Approval is secured for one year only and must be renewed.

Group Mentoring Implementation Plan Requirements

Programs must submit implementation plans to the state office that include the following elements:

- Description of group mentoring locations and a step-by-step plan of how group mentoring will be launched, supervised, and maintained

- A list of students and mentors that will be grouped (if known)

- Explanation of why group mentoring is necessary for a program

Exercise 1: Is Group Mentoring Right for Your Program?

Step 1: Coordinate student locations, schedules, and available spaces.

Take inventory of the students you have at different schools and locations and determine if a group mentoring model could work. Key questions you should answer include the following:

- What schools are currently being served?
- How many students are served at each school?
- Which students have similar lunch schedules?
- What spaces are available and at what times?
- Will the available spaces offer groups privacy for up to six people and a place to eat, such as a large table with chairs where the group can face one another?

Step 2: Assess your program's capacity to launch and monitor group mentoring.

- Does your program have staff who are familiar enough with the students to make appropriate grouping and mentor pairing choices?
- Does your program have a positive established relationship with schools where the group mentoring will take place? (This helps with securing space and ensuring that school leadership is aware of the changes associated with the group mentoring model.)
- Is there significant interest among current staff, mentors, and students to utilize a group mentoring model?
- How likely will it be to find mentors with interest and experience in working with groups of students?

Step 3: Does it all fit?

Review your answers to the above questions. Do your answers contain all of the elements in the below checklist of community readiness must-haves?

Program Readiness Factors for Group Mentoring

✓ Groups of students that can be clustered in school-based or afterschool settings
✓ Access to mentors experienced with managing groups of students
✓ Program staff that can effectively group students based on individual characteristics
✓ Space that can accommodate group meetings and coordinated scheduling efforts

PART 2: RECRUIT AND SCREEN MENTORS

Recruitment for group mentors and individual mentors should happen simultaneously. Mentors should be appropriately screened according to program requirements, schools and partners, and state and federal laws. Mentor screening refers to the process of qualifying volunteers to become mentors. Screening mentors protects students and minimizes your local program's legal risk. Screening mentors also allows you to select the highest quality individuals to mentor your students.

Take Stock in Children adheres to a strict confidentiality policy with the information collected from volunteer mentors. Only designated staff are to have access to mentors' personal information, and files should be kept in a locked cabinet. Mentors have the right to examine and contest information in their files, including their background checks. The information collected from your mentors should only be used for suitability screening, matching, training, and performance evaluation.

It is a Take Stock in Children policy that candidates who knowingly provide false background information with regard to their identity, employment history, residence, or criminal background must be automatically disqualified. There must be a clear sign of the intent to deceive; making a benign mistake, like misspelling a former employer's name, is not grounds for disqualification.

Once a program has a pool of recruited mentors, staff should evaluate the applications to determine if an individual might be a good fit for a group mentoring setting based on their background and experience. (There is no place on the application for the mentor to request working in a group setting.) At this point, staff should approach the potential mentor and ask them if they would be interested in mentoring a group of students.

Group mentors should have previous experience working with students and preferably managing groups of students. Current or former teachers are excellent choices; other examples include leading boy scouts, church youth groups, etc. At one site that was studied during the creation of this manual, teachers at a school were serving as mentors during lunchtime. This was ideal because it helped the mentors know their students better, and the mentors were present in school beyond the session in the event that their students needed to check in with them.

Volunteer Mentor Disqualifiers

- Failure to complete the screening process.

- Past history of sexual abuse.

- Conviction of any crime in which children were involved.

- History of violence or sexually exploitive behavior.

- Termination from a paid or volunteer position caused by misconduct with a child.

Exercise 2: Recruit and Screen Mentors

Step 1: Identify your "mentor gap."

- How many mentors do you need to recruit in order for every student in the program to have an individual mentor?
- How many mentors do you need for all students to have a group mentor?
- Is there a combination of individual and group mentors that would best serve the students in your program?

Step 2: Investigate potential sources of mentors in your community.

- Make a list of businesses, civic organizations, faith-based establishments, etc., that you can target.
- Use your own connections, those of your leadership council and board of directors, and other mentors.
- Spend a concentrated amount of time working out a relationship with an organization that will result in a number of mentors joining the program at one time. (Consider providing on-site recruitment presentations, training, and fingerprinting.)

Step 3: Interview the applicants.

Asking mentors more about themselves and their motivation for volunteering with Take Stock in Children is an effective risk management activity. It is also an opportunity to get to know the volunteers, identify any preconceptions about mentoring that may lead to problems, and review the next steps. Be sure your interview includes the following questions:

- Tell me about your employment history.
- Where were you born? Raised?
- What is your family like?
- Why do you want to mentor?
- What qualities do you like/dislike in kids?
- What expectations do you have for your student(s)?
- What do you think your experience as a mentor will be like?

Step 4: Identify the group mentors

- Examine your recruited mentor pool and determine which applicants fulfill the following:
- Have previous experience working with and managing groups of students in settings such as the classroom, scout groups, church youth groups, etc.

- Use the above interview process in Step 3 to learn more about a potential mentor's experience to see if they are a good fit for a group.
- Approach these mentors and ask them if they would consider mentoring a group of students.

Step 5: Screen mentors

- Perform character reference checks.
- Conduct a Florida Department of Law Enforcement state criminal history information search to find out if a mentor has a criminal history.
- Coordinate with your local school district to ensure that volunteers meet the school district's background screening for mentors.
- Follow your program's policy for offenses that disqualify a mentor.

PART 3: TRAIN MENTORS

Take Stock in Children group mentors can participate in the same training as 1:1 mentors; however as a best practice, it is recommended that programs offer specific group mentor training that provides mentors support around group facilitation. Mentor training refers to the initial and continuous education and support of the adults who volunteer to serve as role models for students. Properly training both group and individual mentors lays the foundation for positive results that stem from mentoring.

Take Stock in Children has several policies in place to ensure mentor training for all types of mentors is completed consistently. Mentor Coordinators are primarily responsible for arranging and delivering mentor training. If no Mentor Coordinator exists, then the Student Services Coordinator should offer the training. When developing and offering mentoring training, programs should ensure that the following steps are taken:

- Every Take Stock in Children mentor must complete an initial mentor training session before being matched with a student.
- Mentors must be provided with a clear explanation of the policies and procedures of in-school mentoring and sign a Mentor Agreement form that outlines these policies and procedures, states that the mentor understands them, and documents his or her agreement to follow them. Training should include an explanation and description of the Program Policies relevant to mentoring.
- Training must include a description of the needs of Take Stock in Children students. Take Stock in Children serves students with a moderate number of risk factors, which must be addressed in the training.
- Take Stock in Children requires that local programs include a Confidentiality Policy component in their initial mentor training session.
- If a local program refers mentors to a third-party organization for mentor training, the above policies must be met before the mentor's first meeting with a student.

- Mentors will be trained to use the Take Stock in Children website to find mentoring resources and tools for them to use with their students.
- If the local program refers mentors to a third-party training center, mentors and/or the third-party training center will be provided with training information specific to Take Stock in Children, including the policy regarding in-school mentoring.

Benefits of Mentor Training

✓ Realistic mentor expectations.

✓ Improved mentor competence and productivity.

✓ Increased mentor retention rates.

✓ Longer-lasting mentor-student relationships.

✓ Better support for students.

✓ Greater mentor satisfaction.

Exercise 3: Provide Effective Mentor Training 4: Conduct Effective Mentor Sessions

Effective mentor training prepares adults to build close, long-lasting relationships by clarifying their role as mentor, teaching them basic mentoring skills, and providing them with tools and resources. Follow the steps in this exercise to help your group mentors approach their mentoring relationships well-resourced and with confidence.

Step 1: Schedule and Conduct Training.

Before the training:

- Secure a suitable training location that has appropriate space, furnishings, equipment and supplies (e.g., audio-visual equipment, chalk or dry erase boards, etc.).
- Select a convenient date and time to maximize attendance.
- Personally contact mentors to notify them of the date, time, and location.
- Develop the activities to use during the training.

During the training:

- Training staff should arrive early to set up the room and materials.
- Welcome mentors to the training and take attendance by utilizing a sign-in sheet.
- Give mentors the option of using the TSIC Mentor Toolkit (excerpts included in Attachment B of this manual) or self-designing a curriculum using the TSIC Guiding Principles outlined above in this section.

· Ask attendees for feedback at the end of the session.

After the training:

· Thank the mentors for their time and continue the process of obtaining security clearances.

· Follow up with trained mentors to answer any questions they may have and to discuss the next part of the onboarding process – matching them with a group of students (see the next section below).

Step 2: Complete the Mentor Training Checklist.

Ensure that the following elements have been addressed through your program's mentor training.

· Have all mentors completed the initial training session before being matched with a student?	☐ Yes ☐ No
· Have mentors been provided with a clear explanation of the policies and procedures of in-school group mentoring?	☐ Yes ☐ No
· Have all mentors signed an agreement stating they understand and agree to follow the policies and procedures?	☐ Yes ☐ No
· Did mentor training include · An explanation of Take Stock in Children Program Policies relevant to mentoring? · A description of the needs of Take Stock in Children students? · A Confidentiality Policy component?	☐ Yes ☐ No

PART 4: TWO PATHWAYS FOR IMPLEMENTATION

Group mentoring is most successful when mentors and students are given the tools that are well matched to their individual needs and experiences. TSIC has found that there is no "one size fits all" approach to a group-mentoring curriculum. In fact, during the data collection process that resulted in this manual, mentors' use of materials varied greatly according to individual experience and preference. The majority of mentors report relying on the structured lessons and activities included in the TSIC Mentor Toolkit to plan their sessions. However, there are other instances where mentors reported digressing from the curriculum in response to specific student needs or times when a topic warrants further deeper discussion and investigation. Therefore, two paths are offered here that mentors can take when choosing content and structure for their sessions. The tools accompanying these paths range from the highly structured TSIC Mentor Toolkit curriculum, which utilizes a set scope and sequence, to the TSIC Mentoring Guiding Principles that mentors can refer to as they build their own sessions. In most cases, mentors take information from both pathways to customize a mentoring experience tailored to the needs of their group.

Mentor Session Implementation Pathways

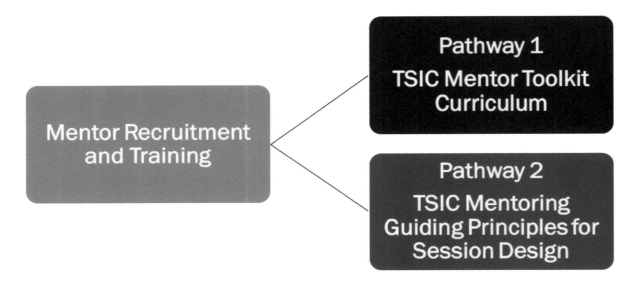

Samples from the TSIC Mentor Toolkit

Attachment B of this manual includes excerpts from the TSIC Mentor Toolkit. To access the Toolkit in its entirety, please go to www.tsic.org.

TSIC Mentoring Guiding Principles

Guiding principles are useful for those mentors who prefer to self-design and structure their own mentor sessions. These guiding principles include step-by-step instructions about how to use best practices as well as lessons learned in order to produce the most effective and impactful mentor sessions possible.

The following guiding principles represent the core mission and goal of TSIC mentoring in both individual and group settings. These principles should be the foundation of all mentoring activities and suggestions. The chapter then discusses how to go about designing and structuring a mentor session with these principles in mind. As part of this discussion, resources and best practices are included for each principle.

Guiding Principle 1: Help your students experience personal growth and development through goal setting, envisioning the future, and defining positive values.

Guiding Principle 2: Support your students' academic success, help them build the skills and strategies they need, and connect them to resources.

Guiding Principle 3: Assist your students in planning for college in high school by monitoring their progress toward post-secondary enrollment.

Guiding Principle 4: Explore careers with your students by giving them practical information about working in the community and becoming motivated and excited about the future.

How to Design a Group Mentor Session

Design Steps

Planning a group-mentoring lesson is very similar to designing a lesson plan that might be implemented in a classroom setting. Mentors should follow these steps when determining what to include in and how to approach a session. Mentors with previous educational experience may have lesson plan development techniques that work for them, but a good rule of thumb is to always produce a written plan as a guide.

1. State the Objective – Mentors should ask themselves what they want their students to learn or gain from the mentoring session. This objective should be directly tied to one of the four guiding principles listed above.

2. Investigate Activity Options – The Internet is a vast resource full of free advice and ideas for conducting effective mentor sessions. The next section offers resources for each guiding principle that can help mentors get started with generating activities. Additionally, Google searches on specific topics can also direct mentors to ideal activities that fit the stated objective.

3. Plan Realistic Timing – One of the most challenging aspects of planning a lesson or mentor session is making sure that the planned activities fit comfortably within the session's timeframe. When timing goes awry, it is usually because too much activity or content was packed into a session.

It's better to end early or plan for an intentional pause so that a topic can be continued next session rather than not getting to the core content of a lesson. This being said, there could be instances where an early part of a discussion leads to an incredibly rich and meaningful conversation that was not planned. In cases like this, mentors use their best judgment about how to revise their plan in response to student need.

Group Mentor Session Structure

Topic: This is the title of your session and should reflect the guiding principle and objective in an abbreviated way.

Objective: This critical piece of planning defines the session and sets the stage for success. No matter how fun or important a session activity is, without a clear objective, it misses the mark.

Guiding Principle: Reference one of the four guiding principles listed in the beginning of the chapter.

Resources/Materials: List all resources and materials needed for a successful session. Nothing is worse than having a well-planed session only to find that important materials are missing when the time comes to use them.

Introduction: Give students a "30,000-foot view" of the session. Tell students what they will be discussing and give an overview of what will be expected of them. This is also an opportunity to activate prior knowledge and find out what students already know.

Main Activity: This is the core of the mentor session and is where you are directly coaching your students. Be sure that whatever activity is chosen reflects what your students know and what you want them to know.

Assessment: Every mentor session should include an informal or anecdotal assessment. This is a way for mentors to check student understanding and find out if additional support is needed.

Closure: Every session should have an opportunity to summarize or wrap up the discussion. Some examples of how this could be done include writing a sentence about what they learned, briefly stating what they liked/disliked about the session, or making suggestions for follow-up topics and activities.

4. Write Down a Plan – The following structure is suggested to help mentors organize and record their plan for a mentor session. It can be used to record the session objective, introduction, main activity, resources and materials, informal assessment, and closure.

How to Support Guiding Principles

The following section offers best practices, ideas, and tips about how to create content and mentoring sessions that align with the Group Mentoring Guiding Principles.

Guiding Principle 1: Help your students experience personal growth and development through goal setting, envisioning the future, and defining positive values.

Activities that reflect this principle might include exploring personal interests, setting realistic short- and long-term goals, and focusing on what lifelong success and happiness means. When searching for and developing activities, look for ones that support the following:

- Goal Setting
- Staying on Track
- Positive Outlook
- Peer Pressure
- Bullying
- Personal Values

The following websites may help mentors continue to explore personal interests and values with the student groups:

- www.viacharacter.org -- A free personality survey that helps individuals evaluate their individual strengths.
- www.kevan.org/johari -- The Johari Window tool allows individuals to draw on feedback from friends and family members in order to create a personality map.
- www.lifevaluesinventory.org – An inventory assessment that identifies students' values and provides tools to explore careers and educational majors aligned with each value (financial prosperity, concern for others, independence, etc.).

Helpful Tips

✓ Try to relate to students by thinking about how you viewed the world at their age.

✓ Find common ground about shared interests that will strengthen your relationship with your students.

✓ Remind students that they are in control of the way they react to a situation and to remain positive when dealing with difficult moments.

✓ Help students identify some positive experiences each week.

Guiding Principle 2: Support your students' academic success and help them build the skills and strategies they need and connect them to resources.

Activities that reflect this principle might focus on basic organizational skills and self-discipline. When searching for and developing activities, look for ones that support the following:

- Learning Styles
- Homework
- Note Taking
- Speed Reading
- Standardized Tests
- Study Habits
- Time Management and Planning

The following websites may help you continue to explore academic skills with your students:

- www.khanacademy.com – Through instructional videos, students pursue self-paced learning about math, art, computer programming, economics, physics, chemistry, biology, medicine, finance, and history.
- www.funbrain.com – Educational activities & games are created for students to reinforce skills learned in school.
- www.familyeducation.com – This site offers the user information about adolescent issues.
- www.powa.org – This instructional site for students offers tips and exercises for improving writing skills.

Helpful Tips

✓ Help your students make using their planners a habit by asking to see them when you visit.

✓ Students should review notes daily. The more they read them, the more they will learn, and the better they will do on a test.

✓ Helping your students prepare for their standardized tests can result in increased confidence and better overall testing performance.

✓ Check registration forms for dates, registration deadlines, instructions, test center codes, and other information.

Guiding Principle 3: Assist your students in academic and financial planning for college in high school by monitoring their progress toward post-secondary enrollment.

Helpful Tips

✓ Discuss various career choices and the education required for them.

✓ Encourage students to research the specific requirements at the schools they are considering attending.

✓ Stress the importance of obtaining as many scholarships as possible.

Activities that reflect this principle might focus on preparing for college and understanding financial aid opportunities. When searching for and developing activities, look for ones that support the following:

- Application Process
- High School vs. College Experiences
- Campus Tours
- College Degrees
- State Colleges

- FAFSA
- Florida Prepaid

The following websites may help you continue to explore college readiness with your students:

- https://studentaid.ed.gov/sa/fafsa/estimate -- This site offers a tool for younger students called the FAFSA4Caster calculator to estimate what financial aid they're eligible for based on current family income.

- www.fafsa.ed.gov – Information about FAFSA preparation and filing is provided.

- www.navigatingyourfinancialfuture.org – This site offers information about FAFSA completion assistance at locations across Florida.

- www.fastweb.com – A free scholarship search helps connect students with resources.

- http://www.floridashines.org/ -- This site has a self-directed college and career search tool.

- www.collegeboard.org and www.act.org -- These sites house college and career exploration alongside test prep and college readiness information.

- www.FSassessments.org – Info about Florida's standardized tests can be found here.

- http://www.floridastudentfinancialaid.org/ – This site details academic requirements for Florida Bright Futures and other scholarships.

- www.fldoe.org/academics/graduation-requirements -- A helpful review of academic requirements for Florida students is published each year. Students are always held to the requirements, which were current in their 9th-grade year

Guiding Principle 4: Explore careers with your students, giving them practical information about working in the community and boosting their motivation and excitement for the future.

Helpful Tips

✓ Many skills learned in school transfer directly to the workplace. Share how you use these skills in the work you do.

✓ Gaining valuable work experience is vital to your students' future.

✓ Share personal job application and interview experiences with students.

Activities that reflect this principle might focus on matching individual interests to career paths and helping students understand all the factors to consider when making a career choice. When searching for and developing activities, look for ones that support the following:

- How to Apply for a Job
- Career Exploration
- Creating a Cover Letter
- Developing a Resume
- Job Interviews
- Workplace Knowledge

The following websites may help you continue to explore careers with your students:

- www.monster.com/career-advice -- Students are provided with examples of current job postings and help to research careers.
- www.careeronestop.org/toolkit -- Employment trends and projections, salary guides, and career exploration tests help students navigate early career readiness.
- http://www.bls.gov/k12/students.htm -- Here, students can see an example of an occupational handbook.
- www.floridashines.org -- This site offers students opportunities to take career assessments and explore career information linked to majors, interests, and skills.

PART 5: GROUP STUDENTS, AND PAIR THEM WITH MENTOR

Once mentors have been vetted and trained, they will need to be assigned to a group of students. The first action in this part of the process is to understand when mentors are available. Staff who have implemented the group-mentoring model report that a good strategy is to ask mentors to select a consistent day/time that they would like to meet with students. When asking them for their preference, it is helpful to let them know if there are particular days that are already busy with groups and then encourage them to fill in the gaps.

Effective student grouping is one of the most critical factors for successful group mentoring experiences. As mentioned above, clustering students in individual schools is important because it ensures that they are already at the mentoring location and allows for lunchtime meetings, which have greater attendance. Also, students are able to see and know one another regularly in the context of their regular school day. Be sure that any students who will be participating in group mentoring have updated TSIC contracts that state they will be receiving either group or individual mentoring.

Student schedules are another primary consideration. If students are meeting at school during lunch, it is important that they have the same lunch period. Next, students should be sorted by gender. It has been reported by staff that gender-specific groups allow students to be more open and honest, especially if they are sharing sensitive issues. Third, students should be grouped according to their grades and behavior.

One staff member reported sorting students based on their academic performance and behavior into three categories: high achieving, "middle of the road," and borderline/low. It is recommended to group the "middle of the road" students with the higher achieving students and the lower students with the middle students if possible. This is the environment that will promote peer influences to help students move up to the next level of achievement.

Finally, a number of additional individual student characteristics should be considered when grouping students, which are listed in Exercise 3. It is essential that the person grouping students has a very comprehensive understanding of them as individuals.

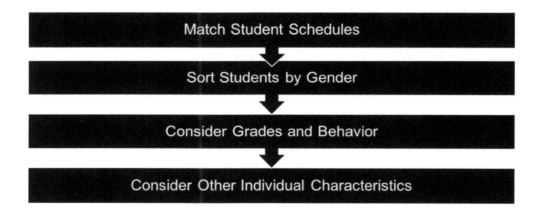

Exercise 4: Match Students and Mentors

Follow the steps below to effectively match groups of students with a mentor.

Step 1: Determine mentor availability.

Step 2: Group students by using the following criteria in order:

- Create groups of students with common lunch schedules.
- Divide each group by gender.
- Refine gender-specific groups by grades and behavior.
- Consider individual student characteristics before finalizing the groupings, according to the chart below, to ensure students are a good fit with one another and their mentor.

Individual Student Characteristics	
Personality	Likes and Interests
Student Social Circles	Home Life/Level of Family Support
Attendance	Teacher Comments
Classroom Performance	Rapport with Peers and Instructors

PART 6: SET EXPECTATIONS AND CONDUCT SESSIONS

Successful group mentoring implementation is built upon setting clear expectations for both students and mentors. For mentors, this expectation-setting occurs during TSIC mentor training. For students, it is recommended that a meeting with program staff and students participating in group mentoring be held prior to their first group mentoring session. The purpose of this first meeting is to review the group mentoring process with students and set expectations about what will happen during the sessions. This is also a time to address any student questions or concerns. Suggested topics to be covered with students include the following:

- Scheduling
- Mentoring session locations
- What to expect during the first and subsequent mentor sessions
- Roles and responsibilities of both the mentor and the students

It is also important during this time to make certain that students understand that while their mentoring is happening in a group setting, they should be comfortable to let their mentor know if there is an issue they are experiencing that they don't want to discuss with the group. This ensures that a student's need for privacy is maintained and that they have the opportunity to receive the same individualized support that they would in a 1:1 setting.

If meeting space is likely to be an issue, let mentors know in advance. For example, if it is likely that mentors and groups will be meeting in a different location session to session, be sure to prepare mentors for this. Create a clear system for communicating session locations with mentors in order to reduce confusion.

For the first mentor session, an affiliate staff member may want to be present at the beginning to review and reinforce the expectations discussed at the initial student meeting with the mentor present (if the affiliate staff member and mentor feel it is necessary). At this meeting, be sure that mentors and students exchange contact information so everyone will be on the same page if mentors or students need to reschedule a session or will be absent.

Exercise 5: Conduct the Initial Student Meeting

Step 1: Schedule an Initial Student Meeting

- Determine a convenient time and location for students to first come together and meet one another.
- If possible, hold the meeting at the regular time and place where the mentoring group will meet.

Step 2: During the Initial Meeting

- Introduce students to one another.
- Review what to expect during mentor sessions.
- Be clear about appropriate behavior and how to effectively participate in the sessions.
- Confirm student schedules, meeting locations, and the importance of good attendance.

Step 3: After the Initial Meeting

- Follow up with students individually to find out if they have any questions, comments, or concerns.
- Be sure that the mentors and students are in communication about their next meeting.
- Plan to attend the first mentoring sessions with mentor and students together, if needed.

PART 7: MONITOR AND REFINE

Programs should maintain frequent contact with newly matched mentors. For the sessions following the first one, affiliate staff should regularly monitor groups and ensure that mentors are entering session data just as individual mentors do. Affiliate staff may want to have regular check-ins with group mentors every month or every other month to ensure that they have the support they need and that the groups are running smoothly. It is important to find out whether the mentor and student(s) are meeting regularly. If they are not, why not? Is it a commitment problem on the part of the mentor? Is there reluctance on the part of the student? Are there scheduling challenges at the school?

Check in with newly matched students as well. Find out whether they like their mentors and whether there are any problems from the students' point of view.

Most issues with newly matched mentors and students can be corrected through intervention. Once a mentor and student pair are progressing satisfactorily, you can reduce the frequency of your contact. Keep track of your contacts with mentor/student matches in the Take Stock in Children database. Develop a timeline for mentor contacts that works for you, and stick to it.

Take Stock in Children requires mentors to sign in and report every student meeting, and local program staff should monitor mentor sign-ins to ensure that mentors are meeting the program standards. You should also have some policy for regular contact with your mentors, both to ensure that they are meeting with their students regularly, and also that they have all of the resources they need to be successful. Your mentor supervision plan should include occasional visits to schools, mentor support events, mentor surveys, and communication via phone, e-mail, newsletter, Facebook, etc. It is important to make it easy for mentors to get in touch with you if they have questions or need assistance. If you do discover that a mentor and student have stopped meeting, do what you can to get them back on track quickly.

If your mentor supervision reveals that a mentor has not been meeting with his or her student, you must first establish whether the mentor wants to continue. Next, you will need to assess the issues that have contributed to the problem. At this point, it is probably appropriate to talk to the mentor and student individually.

It is important that our Take Stock in Children students have a good understanding that our program is not only a scholarship opportunity but also a mentoring program. In order to participate, the student must meet with a mentor at school. However, if there is a conflict between a mentor and student and the student does not feel comfortable with the match, he or she must have the freedom and the opportunity to talk honestly with a Take Stock in Children staff member and to request a new mentor.

Mentor Program Standards

✓ Mentors meet their student two times or more each month during the school year.

✓ Mentors meet with students at least 30 minutes per meeting.

✓ Mentor-student meetings take place only on the school campus or during official TSIC functions.

Some of these issues cause problems in mentor matches:

- Have the mentor and student had issues finding topics of conversation?
- Have the mentor or student missed scheduled meetings?
- Does the student give the impression that he/she is not interested in mentoring? Is that a true impression, or just teenage reserve?
- Are there cultural differences contributing to the mentor's discomfort, like the language that the student uses or the behavior that they discuss?
- Has the mentor expressed disapproval of the student's lifestyle, family, behavior, or choices?

If you believe that the issues can be resolved, schedule and attend a return meeting at the school. Make sure that there are clear lines of communication between the mentor and student, and that they have established a weekly meeting schedule.

While the pair are re-engaging, provide regular supervision and support. Check in frequently until you are confident that the meetings are back on track.

Below is a set of FAQs that can serve as a reference as you work to resolve any issues that may arise with your group mentors as they are conducting their sessions.

PART 8: FREQUENTLY ASKED QUESTIONS

Do I have to use the TSIC Mentor Toolkit?

The Toolkit is a useful guide for any program implementing the group mentoring model. However, you may choose to design your own curriculum using the guiding principles outlined in Part 4 of this manual. However, the policies and procedures included in the manual must be followed.

Scheduling groups is proving to be a challenge. Are there ways to make it easier?

The best times for groups to meet are during free periods or lunch blocks. Find these times at the beginning of the academic year and offer them as options for the mentors.

Scheduling groups can be one of the more challenging aspects of group mentoring. Chapter 2: Part 1: Assess Readiness and Secure Approval has some tips for addressing the scheduling challenge. They include identifying schools that have common school-wide free time built into their week for students to meet, utilizing an embedded staff member effectively, and obtaining class schedules prior to the start of the academic year. Another suggestion from a program was to have a checklist that the students fill out with their availability. They can also use signal vine to get the time they go to lunch.

How big should a group be? Can I have a group with two students?

Group mentoring is defined as at least two students meeting with one mentor. Programs have flexibility to make their group sizes as large or small as they feel is appropriate as long as they receive approval of their Implementation Plan from the President and CEO.

Do I need to submit an implementation plan each year?

Yes, implementation plans need to be revised and submitted each year by the third business day in June to the Take Stock in Children President & CEO to ensure that the TSIC affiliate and school are on the same page about coordinating group mentoring programs.

Are certain times of the year more difficult to hold group mentoring sessions?

Programs report that holding group mentoring sessions during standardized testing periods in the spring can prove challenging. This is due to increased limitations on available space and student time. Often, rooms typically used for group mentoring sessions must be used to store testing materials or testing small groups of students. It is important to understand this schedule and develop alternative arrangements in advance.

What should a mentor do if a student needs to talk to them one-on-one?

While group mentoring provides students with the opportunity to support one another in a group setting, there are times when students have issues they are not comfortable sharing in the group. In these cases, the mentor is encouraged to speak with that student individually and even have a meeting beyond the group setting to work through the issue as needed.

How do mentors indicate that a student was part of a group mentoring session when logging the session in STAR?

For each student, mentors should select the type of mentor session that they are conducting when entering sessions in STAR.

ATTACHMENT A:

Group Mentoring Implementation Plan

Group mentoring is a supplement to individual mentoring and should only be used after this implementation plan has been submitted to the State Office and approved. As you are answering the questions below, please keep in mind that no more than 10% of an affiliate's students in a given school year can use group mentoring. Please submit this plan to the State Office by the third business day of June each year.

1. Program name:	2. Person submitting this plan:	
3. Please describe the site(s) and physical location(s) where group mentoring will occur:		
4. How many students do you anticipate will be group mentored?	5. How many group mentors do you anticipate having?	6. Approximately how many students will be in a group?
7. Please describe how you will identify students and mentors who will use group mentoring. If you have a specific list of participants, please attach it.		
8. Please indicate the planned launch date for your implementation of group mentoring.		
9. Do you anticipate any challenges with securing a location and launching group mentoring? If so, what are they and how will you address them?		

ATTACHMENT B:

Samples from the TSIC Mentor Toolkit

The following five activities are excerpts from the TSIC Mentor Toolkit curriculum that have been identified as appropriate for use with group mentoring. To access the TSIC Mentor Toolkit in its entirety, please go to www.tsic.org.

The included excerpts are:

- Activity 1 – Hot Topics
- Activity 2 – Highs and Lows
- Activity 3 – S.M.A.R.T. Goals
- Activity 4 – My Vision Board
- Activity 5 – What's Going Well

ACTIVITY 1: HOT TOPICS

Learning Objective: Mentees will engage in a meaningful conversation with their adult mentor.

Materials: Copy of "Hot Topics" worksheet, hat or basket, pair of scissors.

Instructions: Cut the conversations topics on the Hot Topics worksheet into squares. Fold each square in half, so that the topic cannot be seen, and place in the hat or basket. Have each mentee select a square, read the topic, and share their response with the group. Remember to set the expectation that everyone's perspective is valid and there is no wrong answer! Time permitting, allow other mentees to weigh in with their perspectives for others topics as well. Be sure to share your own opinions as well.

If you could be the best in the world at something, what would you pick? Why?	Is it better to be a morning person or a night person?	What activity have you always wanted to try but never had the opportunity?	Is it better to be the oldest or youngest member of your family?
If your friends had to describe you in three words, what would they be?	If you could travel anywhere in the world, where would you go? Why?	If you won a million dollars tomorrow, what is the first thing you would do?	Describe your hero. What qualities do you admire most about this person?
Which three items would you take with you to a desert island?	Which color best describes your personality? Why?	What is the best tradition at your school? Why?	What three things are you most grateful for?
If you could meet any famous person, who would you pick and why?	What is the best book you've ever read? Why would you recommend it?	If you could choose your own super power, what you would pick?	Describe your dream job as a teenager? As an adult?
What emoji do you use most? Why?	If you were granted three wishes, what would they be?	Would you rather travel back in time or forward into the future? Why?	Would you vote for year-round school? Why or why not?
If you had to give up your phone, your music, or the internet, what would you give up?	Would you rather go to a co-ed or single-sex school? Why?	If you could rid the world of one thing, what would it be?	If you were invisible for one day, what would you do?

What thoughts and opinions did you and your mentees have in common? Where do you differ? Try to remember what your thoughts might have been at their age. Remember to keep an open mind!

ACTIVITY 2: HIGHS AND LOWS

Learning Objective: Mentees will use listening and speaking strategies to communicate effectively.

Materials: Copy of "Highs and Lows" activity sheet, scissors, pen/pencil.

Instructions: What do your mentees consider "success" and "failure"? What things do they fear the most? These questions are important because they allow you to see things from your mentee's perspective. Cut the phrases below into squares. Then fold each individual square so that the phrase cannot be seen. Have each mentee select one folded square at a time, read the phrase, and discuss their response with the group. Encourage your mentees to focus on accentuating the positive aspects of each answer: Was there a silver lining? An important lesson learned?

My greatest success in life is....	My greatest academic achievement is....
I am proud of....	A situation or experience I wish I could "do over" is....
I most fear....	I would most like to learn....
Something I did that took courage was....	Something I wish I was better at is....
A lesson I learned from a mistake was....	One thing that is hard for me is....

As you discuss, help your mentees recognize their unique strengths and skills. They might not appreciate how their unique characteristics contributed to their successes.

ACTIVITY 3: S.M.A.R.T GOALS

Learning Objective: The student will gain an understanding of the goal-setting process and set appropriate and manageable goals for their stage in life.

Materials: Copies of "S.M.A.R.T. Goals" activity sheet, pen/pencil, sentence strips.

Instructions: Review the content below with your mentees. Work together to craft a SMART goal for your mentoring group. Then have students work on setting their own SMART goals and recording them on sentence strips or in their journals.

S.M.A.R.T. Goals

Goals: what you would like to achieve

Objectives: how you will reach your goals

Specific
Consider writing a goal that is specific, clearly defines what you want, and answers the Who? What? Where? When? and Why? you will achieve it.

Measurable
Establish concrete criteria for measuring your success and progress. To determine if measurable, ask questions like, "How much?" "How many?" "How will I know when I my goal?"

Achievable
Create a realistic path to achievement that includes action steps and objectives. Your goals should push you past your comfort point; however, you should be able to attain them with dedication and commitment.

Relevant
Consider what the purpose of achieving your goal is. Your goals should be important to you and the outcome should have positive impact on your life.

Timely
Use actual numbers, target dates, or specific events to indicate when your goal will be achieved.

Sample S.M.A.R.T. Goal:

I, John Smith, will begin attending XYZ College in Fall 2019. I will begin coursework to achieve a Bachelor's Degree in Criminal Justice by Spring 2024.

Sample Objectives:

I will attend all five sessions of my school's S.A.T. prep course.

I will work with my mentor and parents to complete the FAFSA form by April 1, 2019,

I will get at least a B in my AP Government class and will sign up for AP History next term.

ACTIVITY 4: MY VISION BOARD

Learning Objective: Mentees will create and share a visual illustration of their short- and long-term goals.

Materials: Copies of "My Vision Board" activity sheet; poster board (one per mentee), a variety of old magazines (can ask mentees to bring to session as well), glue, scissors, markers.

Instructions: Sometimes envisioning the things you want is an effective motivator. You can use this activity to help your mentees create a "Vision Board." Ask mentees to cut out pictures from old magazines that represent what they want to achieve in their future. Their pictures could represent a range of goals, including professional, academic, and personal. Then provide each mentee with poster board to create a college of their vision.

To encourage discussion, ask mentees to use the space provided to list the pictures they chose and briefly explain why they chose to include several in their college. When the collages are finished, have them share their posters with the group. Mentors are encouraged to make one as well to share!

PICTURE	EXPLANATION

ACTIVITY 5: WHAT'S GOING WELL

Learning Objective: Mentees will reflect on the week's activities and gain insight and practice on observing and identifying positive experiences.

Materials: Copies of "What's Going Well" worksheet, pencils/pens.

Instructions: Start by giving mentees several minutes to complete the "What's Going Well" worksheet. Then put mentees into pairs, and ask them to share their responses with each other. When one partner is sharing, the other person should listen carefully and respond back with the positive experiences they heard reflected. Time permitting, allow mentees to share their reflections with the group as well. Be sure to share a few of your own, highlighting the positive side or lesson in at least one challenging situation you experienced.

What's Working Well
What was the high point of the week?
Did you get to know anyone a little better this week?
Did you make any major (or even minor!) changes in your life this week?
Did you accomplish any goals this week?
Did you help anyone this week? Did anyone help you?
What decisions/choices did you make this week?
Did you make any plans for future events this week?
What are you most looking forward to next week?

ATTACHMENT C:

Research

The TSIC group mentoring model is grounded in research. A review of recent studies that focus on group-mentoring programs revealed positive impacts for both students and mentors. This review included a look at a Group Mentoring Pilot launched by Summer Search as well as a Partnership4Kids group mentoring program. This review also included Gabriel P. Kuperminc's study of group mentoring, published by the National Mentoring Resource Center.

In January 2017, Summer Search, a national youth development organization focused on helping low-income students enter and complete college, launched a group mentoring pilot program to see if they could successfully help larger numbers of students using a group mentoring model, as compared to their standard 1:1 format. Summer Search's group model had students meeting in groups that included their mentor and 10 to 12 of their fellow students. In addition, students also checked-in with their mentors by phone on a bi-weekly basis.

The Summer Search Group Mentoring Pilot program yielded successful results with both the students they served and the mentors they worked with. One of the most resounding effects they found were students supporting each other as the group mentoring format purposely encouraged strong peer interactions amongst the participants. In each of the sessions, peers got to know each other by discussing and sharing their own learning styles, fears ,and challenges, as well as their successes and dreams for the future. According to the students, the sessions also helped shape and strengthen their identities as college-bound students (Summer Search, 2017). Not only did these group mentoring sessions allow students to develop positive peer interactions and give each student an opportunity to better know themselves, but it also gave the students the support and encouragement they needed to pursue their dreams. One student's comment about the group atmosphere was, "Their encouragement really helped me keep going when I had a lot of doubt" (Summer Search, 2017). Another mentor stated, "The group has had a strong influence on her [student's] desire to go to college" (Summer Search, 2017). Interestingly, the student this mentor was referring to had stated the previous year that she was not going to apply for college, but after a year of involvement in the group mentoring program, she now says, "The group is why I am applying to college . . . I was not going to apply . . . Then, you see other people you know (in the group) applying for college, and you want to be on their level" (Summer Search, 2017).

Mentors who were part of Summer Search's group mentoring pilot program also reported positive impacts. One mentor felt that working with a group of students allowed her to understand the school culture in a much deeper way. In addition, the group-mentoring model allowed her to see how students interact with one another, and this awareness provided more depth to her mentoring relationships with each individual student. Another mentor spoke about "the value of group mentoring as anchored in the network of support that students build for each other and the increased in-person time I get to spend with students in their school and community" (Summer Search, 2017).

Summer Search's Group Mentoring Pilot is in its second of four years, and findings from a mid-point formative evaluation reinforce the students' observations about their group experience. The evaluation shows that students are building close relationships with each other and their mentors. Students reported continuously high levels of group cohesion and that various indicators of positive group dynamics grew as students got to know one another. Also, students exceeded most interim targets for program participation, and attendance rates remain high across multiple years (Summer Search, 2017).

Partnership4Kids (P4K) is a Nebraska-based organization serving at-risk students through volunteer mentors; it is the only organization in Nebraska that has implemented the unique model of group mentoring into their programming (Partnership4Kids, n.d.). The P4K group mentoring model has volunteer mentors working with a small group of three to four students (within a classroom of 25), who meet three times per month for 90 minutes. One of the biggest benefits P4K cites to using the group-mentoring model is the collaborative atmosphere it creates. They note that students are able to feel more at ease by having peer group support, and mentors don't feel pressured to form an instant 1:1 relationship with students. The group dynamic offers both mentor and students the chance to bond naturally over time (Partnership4Kids, n.d.).

The National Mentoring Resource Center provides a review of group mentoring by Gabriel P. Kuperminc from Georgia State University. He points to preliminary evidence, stating the following:

- Group mentoring programs can produce an array of positive outcomes for youth (behavioral, emotional, academic, etc.) and seem to be effective across a wide range of youth participants (ages, ethnicities, etc.).
- Additional relational processes, such as group cohesion and belonging and a strong group identity, may also contribute to the outcomes youth experience from group mentoring.
- Group mentoring programs offer a context for activities that develop student skills, change student attitudes, and offer positive peer interactions; and that these processes may lead to behavioral outcomes for participants (Kuperminc, 2016).

In summary, the successes of these group-mentoring programs, along with Kuperminc's review, point out the benefits that a mentoring organization can expect from a hybrid mentoring model where group mentoring supplements the traditional 1:1 model. These benefits include the following:

- Positive peer interactions, relationship building, and a sense of belonging amongst students.
- Expansion of a supportive and encouraging environment to help students succeed.
- An opportunity for mentors to get to know their students on a deeper level as they interact with others.

ATTACHMENT D:

References

Kuperminc, G.P. (2016). Group Mentoring. Retrieved from
    http://www.nationalmentoringresourcecenter.org/index.php/what-works-in-mentoring/mod-
    el-and-population-reviews.html?id=121

Partnership4Kids. (n.d.). Value of Mentoring. Retrieved from
    http://p4k.org/values/value-of-mentoring/

Summer Search (2017, February 16). Group Mentoring: Benefitting Students and Mentors Alike. Retrieved
    from https://blog.summersearch.org/2017/02/16/group-mentoring-benefitting-
    students-and-mentors-alike/

Tierney, J.P., Grossman, J.B., and Resch, N. (1995). Making a Difference.
    An Impact Study of Big Brothers Big Sisters. (1995).

Take Stock Innovation Collection: Virtual Mentoring

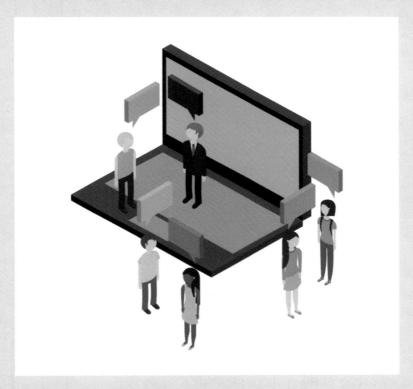

Take Stock in
Children®

The contents of this manual were developed under a grant from the U.S. Department of Education, Investing in Innovation (i3) Program. However, those contents do not necessarily represent the policy of the U.S. Department of Education, and you should not assume endorsement by the federal government.

Table of Contents

ACKNOWLEDGEMENTS

Take Stock in Children (TSIC) would like to thank and acknowledge the UNISON team for working tirelessly to launch and successfully implement the innovations supported by TSIC's Investing in Innovation (i3) grant. This team, led by Judy Saylor, Director of Program Growth and Innovation, includes Tiara Arline, Sara Buckley, Tiffany Givens, Amy Grunder, Roxanne Jordan, and Luz Rodriguez. The i3 grant program is ultimately about reaching scale—taking innovations from pilot to multiple sites and programs. Because of the team's work, innovations will impact over 8,500 students per year through 45 independent affiliates across the TSIC network.

TSIC would also like to give a special thanks to the Take Stock in Children local affiliates, the Immokalee Foundation and the Education Foundation of Collier County – Champions for Learning, who contributed their time and expertise to field test and refine the virtual mentoring model.

TSIC would like to recognize Gary Romano and the Civitas Strategies team for guiding the codification and scaling process of the innovations developed during the i3 grant program.

Finally, a special thank you to Ethan Fieldman, President of Study Edge and Take Stock in Children board member, for generously making GoBoard.com available to the TSIC network.

The increased number of students served and the continually growing demand means that UNISON innovations will provide the network with opportunities that efficiently use resources and maintain a high level of programmatic quality and service delivery. Scaling these elements will not only benefit the TSIC network, but also will accelerate the progress of national scaling efforts. Network-wide adoption will effectively result in additional proof points and data, contributing to a climate conducive to national uptake.

Introduction

The Take Stock in Children (TSIC) model of support is built upon the foundation of positive relationships that students develop with their mentors. The impact that a caring adult can have on a student's academic and social-emotional development has been consistently proven in field-based research. There is strong evidence that a community-based mentoring approach decreases drug and alcohol use, enhances peer and parent-child relationships, increases school attendance, and improves attitudes about and performance in school (Tierney, Grossman and Resch, 1995). These positive outcomes are also illustrated in the outstanding results of TSIC students. Each TSIC child is matched with a caring adult mentor who meets with the student at his/her school for an hour each week. Mentors provide academic and behavioral motivation, guidance, friendship, and support. This effective mentor support has greatly contributed to TSIC's results, with:

96% of Take Stock in Children students graduate high school on time

92% of Take Stock in Children students enter post-secondary education

68% of The Stock in Children Students complete post-secondary education, compared to the state average of 27% for at-risk students in poverty

The overall success of the program, coupled with the increasing numbers of students in need, encourages affiliates to target growth in an effort to increase the number of students served across the organization. However, with growth also comes new challenges, particularly in regard to finding the number of mentors needed to serve the increasing population of students. This is especially true for rural programs.

Therefore, TSIC is looking to alternative forms of mentoring that preserve quality but are also more efficient, promoting higher rates of mentor matching and ultimately serving more students.

Virtual mentoring is an approach that can greatly assist organizations in effectively and efficiently supporting greater numbers of students.

Material covered in this manual includes:

- The definition of virtual mentoring;
- When to use virtual mentoring;
- The benefits of virtual mentoring;
- The challenges of virtual mentoring and how to address them;
- Strategies for e-mentors including first contact and meetings; and
- Tools for virtual mentoring implementation.

Launching any new program can be challenging, regardless of the depth of the protocol. If you have any questions not covered in this manual or general feedback you would like to share, please contact the State Office.

CHAPTER (**1**) Why Virtual Mentoring? Definition

Virtual mentoring is a limited-use supplement to the 1:1 adult-student support model where participants rely on electronic tools to communicate for some meetings. For Take Stock in Children, supervised video conferencing through GoBoard.com is the only approved method for virtual mentoring. Virtual mentoring is based on a mutually beneficial relationship between a mentor and a student, with the mentor providing the student with knowledge, advice, encouragement, and modeling. Virtual mentoring is intended to be used only in cases where schedules do not permit face-to-face mentoring throughout the school year. Virtual mentoring should only supplement in-person mentoring, with mentors conducting at least nine in-person, face-to-face sessions per year. The number of pairs using virtual mentoring is limited, as this form of mentoring is not meant to replace the in-person model that has made Take Stock in Children so successful. The State Office will approve the number of virtual mentors for each affiliate on a case-by-case basis.

While a number of differences exist between virtual mentoring and in-person mentoring, a number of crucial similarities do as well.

Characteristics of Virtual Mentoring

- ✓ Meetings are 1:1 between a mentor and student.
- ✓ Goboard.com is used for video calls to facilitate mentor-student contact when an in-person visit is not possible.
- ✓ Sessions are recorded using Goboard.com.
- ✓ Pairs meet at a minimum of 2x per month for 30 minutes.
- ✓ Students must participate in a supervised school or TSIC-sanctioned setting.
- ✓ Online sessions are initiated and supervised by designated program staff.
- ✓ The number of pairs using virtual mentoring is limited, and the State Office must approve the percentage of an affiliate's mentors using the model.
- ✓ For any pair using virtual mentoring, at least nine mentoring sessions should be in person.
- ✓ Virtual mentoring implementation plan must be submitted by programs and approved by the State Office.

TSIC In-Person Mentoring vs. Virtual Mentoring

In-Person Mentoring	Virtual mentoring
Mentors are matched 1:1 with students	Mentors could possibly be matched with more than one student.
Mentors meet in person with students once a week at designated sites.	Geographical boundaries are mitigated as mentors communicate remotely, at least once a week, with their assigned students
Student participants are currently in middle or high school.	
Mentors work with students to provide on-going support to improve college readiness.	
Mentor training and curriculum resources geared toward 1:1 mentoring is used for both in-person and virtual mentoring.	

Benefits of Virtual Mentoring

Sites that have piloted the virtual mentoring approach report several key benefits:

Removal of Barriers to Regular Contact — Virtual mentoring allows mentor-student relationships to occur consistently, even when geographical, time, or financial constraints hinder in-person meetings. Furthermore, virtual mentoring has low barriers to entry, requiring only Internet access and GoBoard to facilitate and record sessions.

Opportunity for More Diverse Mentors — Since the scheduling and geographic concerns associated with in-person face-to-face mentoring relationships/programs are minimized, more mentors can participate.

This diversity can help expose students to mentors in a variety of careers in regional locations (e.g., female students may gain access to women role models in certain career fields who may not otherwise be present in the context of their high schools, neighborhoods, or families).

Increased Mentor Match Rate — Geographical barriers and the consistent time commitment are the two greatest deterrents for potential adult volunteers otherwise interested in mentoring. Virtual mentoring resolves these issues, effectively increasing the rate of mentor recruitment and matching. Also, GoBoard doesn't require advanced hardware beyond a desktop, laptop computer, tablet, or other device. Most new devices have built-in web cameras, and for those not equipped, a small web video device is reasonably affordable.

Challenges of Virtual Mentoring

While clear benefits make virtual mentoring a positive solution for many programs looking to boost their mentor pool while maintaining quality services, several challenges need consideration:

Potential for Miscommunication — While online communication is efficient, it can also invite misunderstanding. When virtual mentoring, being considerate and thoughtful about communication is key since the persons are not in the same room. It may take some targeted effort to overcome the digital divide. Technical issues, such as limited sound quality, broadband issues causing downtime, and connectivity issues, can also negatively impact communication.

Need for Technical Literacy — While the GoBoard is straightforward, mentors and students must have some basic technical skills. Older individuals or people without access to computers may find the concept of virtual mentoring intimidating or outside of their comfort zone of 1:1 communication.

Ensuring Proper Supervision and Security — Virtual mentor-student relationships are subject to the same Take Stock in Children policies and procedures as in-person pairings. However, the Internet is vast, and regulation of contact can be difficult. To ensure that online communication between mentors and students is appropriate, programs must take extra steps to ensure that online video access is taking place during school sessions only, and that all contact is initiated and supervised by Take Stock in Children staff members or designated school staff acting as Take Stock in Children school liaisons. Additionally, all sessions must be recorded and stored in the GoBoard.com system.

Navigating School District Policies – While virtual mentoring can remove barriers to regular contact, related challenges can arise. GoBoard is an accessible platform, however, and the tool has to conform with school district policies. Many districts have restrictions for this type of communication, and a plan of permission and process through each district needs to be navigated and approved before a virtual communication system can be put in place.

CHAPTER (2) Launching Virtual Mentoring

| 1. Assess Readiness and Secure Approval | 2. Recruit and Screen Mentors | 3. Train Mentors | 4. Set Expectations and Conduct Sessions | 5. Monitor and Refine |

Overview of Virtual Mentoring Implementation

For any organization interested in establishing a successful virtual mentoring model, five specific steps should be taken to ensure model fidelity and implementation of best practices. These steps are included in the figure below and explained in greater detail throughout this section.

PART 1: ASSESS READINESS AND SECURE APPROVAL

Virtual mentoring can be a highly effective way to connect more mentors and students across geographies. However, your program's success with launching and implementing virtual mentoring is the direct result of thoughtful preparation and planning. The first step in this process is to ensure that your program has certain readiness factors necessary to launch a successful virtual mentoring program.

Location and Logistics — First, it is crucial to ensure that a suitable location is available for virtual mentoring to take place. For example, a computer lab in a school setting is ideal, as this setting allows students to connect with their mentors while being easily supervised by a program staff member. For efficiency, it is helpful to focus efforts in a school where multiple Take Stock in Children students attend. This allows staff the ability to offer common times where multiple students could be meeting with their mentors in a computer lab setting.

Technology Requirements — Programs should ensure that students and mentors have access to the following software and hardware elements:

- Computer or connected device (laptop, desktop, or tablet)
- Microphone (built-in or external)
- Headphones
- GoBoard.com (TSIC's mandated virtual mentoring platform)

Staff — As with in-person, 1:1 mentoring, student safety and security are critical. Therefore, Take Stock in Children has put strict regulations in place to ensure that mentor-student online contact is appropriate and only occurring during sanctioned times under staff supervision. Programs need to ensure that there are TSIC staff members or designated school liaisons available and present in the room during all online mentoring sessions. TSIC or designated school staff members should be responsible for logging students in and initiating the mentor session. Also, each mentoring session should be recorded using GoBoard.com. Finally, staff should also be responsible for helping students address any technical issues, such as connectivity and sound quality, that may occur during the session.

The diagram below illustrates the typical progression of a TSIC virtual mentoring session:

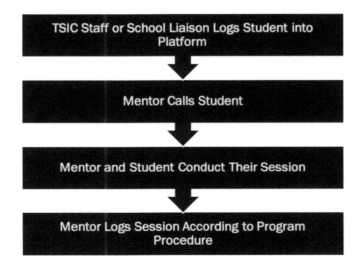

Exercise 1: Is Virtual Mentoring Right for Your Program?

Step 1: Coordinate available spaces and technology requirements.

Take inventory of the students you have at different schools and locations and determine if a virtual mentoring model could work. Key questions you should answer include the following:

- What schools are currently being served?
- Does that school have any policies that may prohibit virtual mentoring or online activity?
- How many students are served at each school?
- Are there available spaces at each school that meet the technical requirements and can serve as a "safe place" for mentoring sessions to occur?
- Is Internet connectivity reliable at the mentoring site?
- Are there students that have similar lunch schedules?

Step 2: Assess your program's capacity to launch and monitor virtual mentoring.

- Does your program have TSIC or designated school staff who can be present to monitor and record virtual mentoring sessions?
- Does your program have a positive established relationship with schools where the virtual mentoring will take place? (This helps with securing space and ensuring that school leadership is aware of the changes associated with the virtual mentoring model.)
- Is there significant interest among current staff, mentors, and students to utilize a virtual mentoring model?
- How likely will it be to find mentors with interest in mentoring via video conferencing?

Step 3: Does it all fit? Review your answers to the above questions. Do your answers contain all of the elements in the below checklist of community readiness must-haves?

Program Readiness Factors for Virtual Mentoring

- ✓ School district allows virtual mentoring and has approved the model
- ✓ Mentoring sites that allow online interaction between students and mentors
- ✓ Access to mentors willing to meet with students online and comfortable with the technical requirements
- ✓ Program staff who can effectively monitor virtual mentoring sessions
- ✓ Space with the technical requirements that can accommodate scheduling efforts

Securing Approval — Virtual mentoring is a supplement to in-person mentoring, but even if a site deems itself ready per this process, it should not begin until it has proposed an implementation plan that has been approved by both the State Office and the school district. Implementation plans must be submitted to the State Office by the third business day in June each year. The number of pairs using virtual mentoring is limited. Affiliates must secure State Office approval for the number of pairings that use virtual mentoring to supplement in-person sessions. The percentage of virtual mentors for each affiliate will be approved on a case-by-case basis. Below are the virtual mentoring implementation plan requirements that Take Stock in Children has set forth. Also, mentors must conduct at least nine in-person, face-to-face sessions per year. Once this requirement has been satisfied, the rest may be virtual.

Implementation plans must be updated and submitted each year (by the third business day in June). Approval is secured for one year only and must be renewed.

Virtual Mentoring Implementation Plan Requirements

Programs must submit implementation plans to the State Office that include the following elements:

- Description of mentoring locations.

- Confirmation that virtual mentoring is allowed at school sites and complies with district and school policy.

- A list of students and mentors that will be virtual (if known) or the anticipated number of pairs.

- Description of how supervision will be maintained during all mentor sessions by TSIC staff or school liaisons (i.e., how will your program ensure that the mentoring location is a "safe space"?).

- Explanation of why virtual mentoring is necessary for a program.

PART 2: RECRUIT AND SCREEN MENTORS

Virtual mentors must have already met all the requirements for being a TSIC mentor, including being appropriately screened according to program requirements, schools and partners, and state and federal laws. Mentor screening refers to the process of qualifying volunteers to become mentors. Screening mentors protects students and minimizes your local program's legal risk. Screening mentors also allows you to select the highest quality individuals to mentor your students.

Take Stock in Children adheres to a strict confidentiality policy with the information collected from volunteer mentors. Only designated staff are to have access to mentors' personal information; files should be kept in a locked cabinet. Mentors have the right to examine and contest information in their files, including their background checks. The information collected from your mentors should only be used for suitability screening, matching, training, and performance evaluation.

It is a Take Stock in Children policy that candidates who knowingly provide false background information with regard to their identity, employment history, residence, or criminal background must be automatically disqualified. There must be a clear sign of the intent to deceive; benign mistakes, such as mis-spelling a former employer's name, is not grounds for disqualification.

Staff should identify and evaluate potential virtual mentors. Selection should be based on the mentor's background and experience, comfort with technology, and the need to use virtual mentoring to supplement in-person sessions. Additionally, the assessment should consider the availability of staff to monitor sessions and the ability to access technology in appropriate locations.

Volunteer Mentor Disqualifiers

- Failure to complete the screening process.

- Past history of sexual abuse.

- Conviction for any crime in which children were involved.

- History of violence or sexually exploitive behavior.

- Termination from a paid or volunteer position caused by misconduct with a child.

Exercise 2: Select Virtual Mentors

Step 1: Identify your "mentor gap."

- Identify mentors who will be able to provide additional sessions if only required to do nine in-person sessions with the rest being virtual.

Step 2: Determine suitability

- Examine identified potential virtual mentors and determine if:
- Mentors and students are willing and able to use technology to supplement in-person mentoring.
- If the student's school has access to appropriate technology and space.
- If the affiliate staff will be available to supervise sessions as required.

Step 3: Select mentors

- Select mentors to participate in virtual mentoring. (Remember, this percentage of mentors needs to be approved by the State Office. Approval of the number of mentors using the model is made on a case-by-case basis.)
- Affiliates may want to keep some virtual mentoring slots "in reserve" for later in the school year (e.g., this will allow you to accommodate a mentor who has a change of schedule and needs to start doing some virtual sessions).

PART 3: TRAIN MENTORS

TSIC virtual mentors participate in the same training as 1:1 mentors. Mentor training refers to the initial and continuous education and support of the adults who volunteer to serve as role models for students. Properly training both virtual and in-person mentors will lay the foundation for the positive results that stem from mentoring.

Take Stock in Children has several policies in place to ensure mentor training for all types of mentors is completed consistently. Mentor Coordinators are primarily responsible for arranging and delivering mentor training. If no Mentor Coordinator exists, the Program Coordinator should offer the training. When developing and offering mentor training, programs should ensure that the following steps are taken:

- Every Take Stock in Children Mentor must complete an initial mentor training session before being matched with a student.
- Mentors must be provided with a clear explanation of the policies and procedures of in-school mentoring and sign a Mentor Agreement form that outlines these policies and procedures, states the mentor understands them, and documents his or her agreement to follow them. Training should include an explanation and description of the Program Policies relevant to mentoring.
- Training must include a description of the needs of Take Stock in Children students. Take Stock in Children serves students with a moderate number of risk factors, which must be addressed in the training.

- Take Stock in Children requires that local programs include a Confidentiality Policy component in their initial mentor training session.
- If a local program refers mentors to a third-party organization for mentor training, the above policies must be met before the mentor's first meeting with the student.
- Mentors will be trained to use the Take Stock in Children website to find mentoring resources and tools for their students.
- If the local program refers mentors to a third-party training center, mentors and the third-party training center should be provided with training information specific to Take Stock in Children, including the policy regarding in-school mentoring.

Benefits of Mentor Training

- Realistic mentor expectations.
- Improved mentor competence and productivity.
- Increased mentor retention rates.
- Longer-lasting mentor-student relationships.
- Better support for students.
- Greater mentor satisfaction.

Training Specific to Virtual Mentoring

In addition to their mentoring training, virtual mentors will receive training using State Office or local program presentations to provide an understanding of program roles, the roles they can play in their student's life, what to expect from the process, how to prepare for mentoring sessions, and how to handle various situations that may arise during their time with their student. They should also be familiar with a few additional policies and procedures specific to the virtual mentor experience. The staff member conducting the training should:

- Ensure that mentors have an active GoBoard account and the required software and hardware for conducting smooth sessions.
- Review student privacy rules with mentors. Mentors are not to have online contact with students beyond the confines of the official mentoring sessions. (Take Stock in Children staff members should be present during the student mentoring sessions and will enter student credentials to begin the GoBoard call.)
- Answer any additional questions that mentors may have about the specifics of virtual mentoring.
- Review Attachment B, which includes excerpts from the TSIC Mentor Toolkit that have been identified as appropriate for use with virtual mentoring.

Two Pathways for Implementation

Virtual mentoring is most successful when mentors and students are given the tools that are well matched to their individual needs and experiences. TSIC has found that there is no "one size fits all" approach to a virtual-mentoring curriculum. In fact, during the data collection process that resulted in this manual, mentors' use of materials varied greatly according to individual experience and preference. Therefore, two paths are offered here that mentors can take when choosing content and structure for their sessions. The tools accompanying these paths range from the highly structured TSIC Mentor Toolkit curriculum with a set scope and sequence, to the TSIC Mentoring Guiding Principles that mentors can refer to as they build their sessions. In most cases, mentors take information from both pathways to customize a mentoring experience that is tailored to the needs of their student.

Mentor Session Implementation Pathways

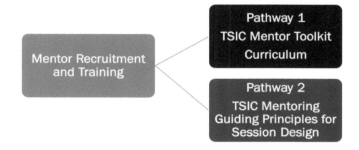

Virtual Mentor Toolkit

Attachment B of this manual provides excerpts from the TSIC Mentor Toolkit that have been identified as appropriate for virtual mentoring. To access the TSIC Mentor Toolkit in its entirety, please go to www.tsic.org.

TSIC Mentoring Guiding Principles

Guiding principles are useful for those mentors who prefer to self-design and structure their own mentor sessions. These guiding principles include step-by-step instructions about how to use best practices and lessons learned to produce the most effective and impactful mentor sessions possible.

The following guiding principles represent the core mission and goal of Take Stock in Children mentoring. These principles should be the foundation of all mentoring activities and suggestions. The section then discusses how to go about designing and structuring a mentor session with these principles in mind. As part of this discussion, resources and best practices are included for each principle.

Guiding Principle 1: Help your students experience personal growth and development through goal setting, envisioning the future, and defining positive values.

Guiding Principle 2: Support your students' academic success and help them build the skills and strategies they need as you connect them to resources.

Guiding Principle 3: Assist your students in planning for college in high school by monitoring their progress toward post-secondary enrollment.

Guiding Principle 4: Explore careers with your students by giving them practical information about working in the community and making them motivated and excited about the future.

How to Design a Mentor Session

Planning a mentoring lesson is very similar to designing a lesson plan that might be implemented in a classroom setting. Mentors should follow these steps when determining what to include in and how to approach a session. Mentors with previous educational experience may have lesson plan development techniques that work for them, but a good rule of thumb is to always produce a written plan as a guide.

1. State the Objective — Mentors should ask themselves what they want their student to learn or gain from the mentoring session. This objective should be directly tied to one of the four guiding principles listed above.

2. Investigate Activity Options — The Internet is a vast resource full of free advice and ideas for conducting effective mentor sessions. The next section offers resources for each guiding principle that can help mentors get started with generating activities. However, Google searches on specific topics can also direct mentors to ideal activities that fit the stated objective.

3. Plan Realistic Timing — One of the most challenging aspects of planning a lesson or mentor session is making sure that the planned activities fit comfortably within the session's timeframe. When timing goes awry, it is usually because too much activity or content was packed into a session. It is better to end early or plan for an intentional pause so a topic can be continued next session than to not get to the lesson's core content. However, in instances where perhaps an early part of the discussion leads to an incredibly rich and meaningful yet unplanned conversation, mentors should use their best judgment about how to revise their plan in real-time in response to student need.

4. Write Down a Plan — The following structure is suggested to help mentors organize and record their plan for each mentor session. It can be used to record the session objective, introduction, main activity, resources and materials, informal assessment, and closure.

Mentor Session Structure

Topic: This is the title of your session and should reflect the guiding principle and objective in an abbreviated way.

Objective: This critical piece of planning defies the session and sets the stage for success. No matter how fun or important a session activity is, without a clear objective, it misses the mark.

Guiding Principle: Reference one of the four guiding principles listed in the beginning of the chapter.

Resources/Materials: List all resources and materials needed for a successful session. Nothing is worse than having a well-planed session only to find that important materials are missing when the time comes to use them. (For e-mentors, physical materials are not possible, so plan activities accordingly.)

Introduction: Give your student an overview of the session. Describe what you will be discussing and give an outline of what is expected. This is also an opportunity to activate prior knowledge and find out what your student already knows about your given topic.

Main Activity: This is the core of the mentor session, where you are providing direct coaching to your student. Be sure that whatever activity is chosen reflects what your student knows and what you want him or her to internalize.

Assessment: Every mentor session should include an informal or anecdotal assessment built into it. This is a way for mentors to check student understanding and find out if additional support is needed.

Closure: Every session should have an opportunity to summarize or wrap up their discussion. Some examples of how this could be done include writing a sentence about what they learned; briefly stating what they liked/disliked about the session; or making suggestions for follow-up topics and activities

How to Support Guiding Principles

The following section offers best practices, ideas, and tips about how to create content and mentoring sessions that align with the Mentoring Guiding Principles.

Guiding Principle 1: Help students experience personal growth and development through goal setting, envisioning the future, and defining positive values.

Activities that reflect this principle might include exploring personal interests, setting realistic short- and long-term goals, and focusing on what lifelong success and happiness means. When searching for and developing activities, look for ones that support the following:

- Goal setting
- Staying on Track
- Positive Outlook
- Peer Pressure
- Bullying
- Personal Values

The following websites may help mentors continue to explore personal interests and values with students:

- www.viacharacter.org -- A free personality survey that helps individuals evaluate their individual strengths.
- www.kevan.org/johari -- The Johari Window tool allows individuals to draw on feedback from friends and family members in order to create a personality map.
- www.lifevaluesinventory.org -- An inventory assessment that identifies students' values and provides tools to explore careers and educational majors aligned with each value (financial prosperity, concern for others, independence, etc.).

Helpful Tips

✓ Try to relate to students by thinking about how you viewed the world at their age.

✓ Finding common ground about shared interests that will strengthen your relationship with your students.

✓ Remind students that they are in control of the way they react to a situation and to remain positive when dealing with difficult moments.

✓ Help students identify some positive experiences each week.

Guiding Principle 2: Support your student's academic success, help build the skills and strategies needed, and connect them to resources.

Activities that reflect this principle might focus on basic organizational skills and self-discipline. When searching for and developing activities, look for ones that support the following:

- Learning Styles
- Homework
- Note-taking
- Speed Reading
- Standardized Tests
- Study Habits
- Time Management and Planning

The following websites may help you continue to explore academic skills with your student:

- www.khanacademy.com – Through instructional videos, students pursue self-paced learning about math, art, computer programming, economics, physics, chemistry, biology, medicine, finance, and history.

- www.funbrain.com -- Educational activities and games are created for students to reinforce skills learned in school.
- www.familyeducation.com -- This site offers the user information about adolescent issues.
- www.powa.org This instructional site for students offers tips and exercises for improving writing skills.

Guiding Principle 3: Assist your student in planning for college by monitoring progress toward post-secondary enrollment.

Activities that reflect this principle might focus on preparing for college and understanding financial aid opportunities. When searching for and developing activities, look for ones that support the following:

- Application Process
- High School vs. College Experiences
- Campus Tours
- College Degrees
- State Colleges
- FAFSA
- Florida Prepaid

Helpful Tips

✓ Help your students create the habit of using their planners by asking to see them when you visit.

✓ Students should review class notes daily. The more they read them, the more they will learn and the better they will do on a test.

✓ Helping your students prepare for their standardized tests can result in increased confidence and better overall testing performance.

✓ Check registration forms for dates, registration deadlines, instructions, test center codes, and other information.

The following websites may help you continue to explore college readiness with your student:

- https://studentaid.ed.gov/sa/fafsa/estimate -- This site offers a tool for younger students called the FAFSA4Caster calculator to estimate what financial aid they're eligible for, based on current family income
- www.fafsa.ed.gov -- Information about FAFSA preparation and filing is provided.
- www.navigatingyourfinancialfuture.org -- This site offers information about FAFSA completion assistance at locations across Florida.
- www.fastweb.com -- A free scholarship search helps connect students with resources.
- www.floridashines.org -- This site has a self-directed college and career search tool.
- www.collegeboard.org & www.act.org -- These sites house college and career exploration, alongside test prep and college readiness information.

- www.FSassessments.org -- Information about Florida's standardized tests can be found here.
- www.floridastudentfinancialaid.org -- This site details academic requirements for Florida Bright Futures and other scholarships.
- www.fldoe.org/academics/graduation-requirements -- A helpful review of academic requirements for Florida students is published each year. Students are always held to the requirements current in their 9th-grade year

Guiding Principle 4: Explore careers with your student, giving them practical information about working in the community and boosting their motivation and excitement about the future.

Activities that reflect this principle might focus on matching individual interests to career paths and helping students understand all the factors to consider when making a career choice. When searching for and developing activities, look for ones that support the following:

- How to Apply for a Job
- Career Exploration
- Creating a Cover Letter
- Developing a Resume
- Job Interviews
- Workplace Knowledge

Helpful Tips

✓ Discuss various career choices and the education required for them.

✓ Encourage students to research the specific requirements at the schools they are considering attending.

✓ Stress the importance of obtaining as many scholarships as possible.

The following websites may help you continue to explore careers with your student:

- www.monster.com/career-advice -- Students are provided with examples of current job postings and receive help to research careers.
- www.careeronestop.org/toolkit -- Employment trends and projections, salary guides, and career exploration tests help students navigate early career readiness.
- http://www.bls.gov/k12/students.htm -- Here, students can see an example of an occupational handbook.
- www.floridashines.org -- This site offers students opportunities to take career assessments and explore career information linked to majors, interests, and skills.

Exercise 3: Provide Effective Virtual Mentor Training

Effective mentor training prepares adults to build close, long-lasting relationships by clarifying their role as mentor, teaching them basic mentoring skills, and providing them with tools and resources. Follow the steps in this exercise to help your virtual mentors approach their mentoring relationships well-resourced and with confidence.

Step 1: Schedule and Conduct Training.

Before the training:

- Schedule a call using GoBoard.com so virtual mentors can test their online access to the meeting.
- Select a convenient date and time to maximize attendance.
- Personally contact mentors to notify them of the date, time, and access information.
- Develop any activities to use during the training.
- Mail a printed copy of the Virtual Mentor Toolkit.

During the training:

- Welcome mentors to the training and take attendance.
- Provide mentors with the TSIC Mentor Toolkit (excerpts included as Attachment B of this manual).
- At the end of the session, ask attendees for feedback through a brief survey.

After the training:

- Thank the mentors for their time and continue the process of obtaining security clearances.
- Follow up with trained mentors to answer any questions they may have.

Step 2: Complete the Mentor Training Checklist.

Ensure that your program's mentor training has addressed the following elements:

- Have all mentors completed the initial virtual mentoring training session before being matched with a student?　　☐ Yes　☐ No

- Have virtual mentors been provided with a clear explanation of the policies and procedures of virtual mentoring?   ☐ Yes ☐ No

- Have virtual mentors signed an agreement stating they understand and agree to follow the policies and procedures?   ☐ Yes ☐ No

Did virtual mentor training include the following: ☐ Yes ☐ No

- An explanation of Take Stock in Children Program Policies relevant to mentoring?
- A description of the needs of Take Stock in Children students?
- A Confidentiality Policy component?

PART 4: SET EXPECTATIONS AND CONDUCT SESSIONS

Successful virtual mentoring implementation is built upon setting clear expectations for both students and mentors. For mentors, this level setting occurs during Take Stock in Children mentor training. For students, it is recommended that a meeting with program staff and students participating in virtual mentoring be held prior to their first virtual mentoring session. The purpose of this first meeting is to review the virtual mentoring process with students and set expectations about what will happen during the sessions. This is also a time to address any student questions or concerns. Suggested topics to be covered with students include the following:

- Scheduling
- Mentoring session locations and technical procedures
- What to expect during the first and subsequent mentor sessions
- Roles and responsibilities of both the mentor and the students

At the beginning of the first mentor session, an affiliate staff member may want to review and reinforce the expectations discussed at the initial student meeting, if the staff member and mentor feel it necessary. At this meeting, be sure that mentors and students exchange contact information in the event that mentors or students need to reschedule a session.

Exercise 4: Conduct the Initial Virtual Session

Step 1: Schedule an Initial Virtual Meeting

- Determine a convenient time and location for a supervised session.

Step 2: During the Initial Meeting

- Introduce the virtual mentoring process.
- Review what to expect during mentor sessions.
- Be clear about appropriate behavior and how to effectively participate in the sessions.
- Confirm the schedule and location (for the student).

Step 3: After the Initial Meeting

- Follow up with the mentor and student individually to find out if they have any questions, comments, or concerns.
- Be sure that mentors, students, and supervising staff are clear about the time and location of the next meeting.

PART 5: MONITOR AND REFINE

Programs should maintain frequent contact with virtually matched mentors. For the sessions following the first one, affiliate staff or school liaisons should continue to always supervise sessions. Affiliate staff may want to have regular check-ins with virtual mentors every month or every other month to ensure they have the support they need and that the virtual mentor sessions are running smoothly.

Program staff should note whether the mentor and student are meeting regularly. If they are not, why not? Is it a commitment problem on the part of the mentor? Reluctance on the part of the student? Scheduling challenges at the school?

Check in with matched students as well. Find out whether they like their mentor and whether any problems exist from the student's point of view with virtual mentoring.

Most issues with matched mentors and students can be corrected through intervention. Once a mentor and student pair are progressing satisfactorily, you can reduce the frequency of your contact. Keep track of your contacts with mentor/student matches in the Take Stock in Children database. Develop a timeline for mentor contacts that works for you and stick to it.

Take Stock in Children requires mentors to sign in at every student meeting, and local program staff should monitor mentor sign-ins to ensure that mentors are meeting the program standards.

You should also have some policy for regular contact with your mentors, both to ensure that they are meeting with their students regularly and also that they have all of the resources they need to be successful. Your mentor supervision plan should include mentor support events, mentor surveys, and communication via phone, e-mail, newsletter, Facebook, etc. Make it easy for mentors to get in touch with you if they have questions or need assistance. If you do discover that a mentor and student have stopped meetings, do what you can to get them back on track quickly.

It is important that our Take Stock scholars have a good understanding that the program is not only a scholarship opportunity, but also a mentoring program. In order to participate, the student must attend their virtual mentoring sessions at school. However, if a conflict occurs between a mentor and student and the student feels uncomfortable with the match, he or she should speak with a Take Stock in Children staff member to request a new mentor.

The following questions can help determine the nature of mentor-student relationship difficulties.

- Have the mentor and student had trouble finding topics of conversation?
- Have the mentor or student missed scheduled meetings?
- Does the student give the impression that he/she is not interested in mentoring? Is that a true impression or just teenage reserve?
- Are there cultural differences contributing to the mentor's discomfort, like the language that the student uses or the behaviors they discuss?

- Has the mentor expressed disapproval of the student's lifestyle, family, behavior, or choices?

If you believe the issues can be resolved, schedule and attend a return meeting at the school. Make sure that there are clear lines of communication between the mentor and student.

While the pair is reengaging, provide regular supervision and support. Check in frequently until you are confident that the meetings are back on track.

Below is a set of FAQs that can serve as a reference as you work to resolve issues that may arise with your mentors as they conduct their sessions.

Mentor Program Standards

✓ Mentors meet their student two times or more each month during the school year.

✓ Mentors meet with students at least 30 minutes per meeting.

✓ Virtual mentor-student meetings take place only when the student is on the school campus or during official TSIC functions.

PART 6: FREQUENTLY ASKED QUESTIONS

Do I have to use the TSIC Mentor Toolkit?

The Toolkit is a useful guide for any program implementing the group mentoring model. However, you may choose to design your own curriculum using the guiding principles outlined in Part 3 of this manual.

However, the policies and procedures included in the manual must be followed.

Do I need to submit an implementation plan each year?

Yes, implementation plans need to be revised and submitted each year to the Take Stock in Children President & CEO to ensure that the TSIC affiliate and school are on the same page about coordinating virtual mentoring programs.

What platform do I need to use to facilitate virtual mentoring?

GoBoard is TSIC's mandated virtual mentoring platform. If another video conference platform is preferred, the President and CEO will approve on a case-by-case basis. Regardless of which platform is used, the staff supervisory requirements remain the same, and the sessions must be recorded, stored, and able to be accessed by the TSIC State Office.

How do mentors indicate that a mentoring session is virtual when entering information into STAR?

When logging a virtual mentor session for each student, mentors should select the option that indicates a session was virtual.

ATTACHMENT A:

Virtual Mentoring Implementation Plan

Virtual mentoring is a limited-use supplement to the 1:1 adult-student support model, in which participants rely on electronic tools to communicate for some meetings. For Take Stock in Children, supervised and recorded video conferencing through GoBoard.com is the only approved method for virtual mentoring. Virtual mentoring is based on a mutually beneficial relationship between a mentor and student, with the mentor providing the student with knowledge, advice, encouragement, and modeling. Virtual mentoring is intended to be used only in cases where schedules do not permit face-to-face mentoring throughout the school year.

Virtual mentoring should only supplement in-person mentoring, with mentors conducting at least nine in-person, face-to-face sessions per year. The number of pairs using virtual mentoring is limited, as this form of mentoring is not meant to replace the in-person model that has made Take Stock in Children so successful. The State Office will approve the number of virtual mentors for each affiliate on a case-by-case basis.

1. Program name:	2. Person submitting this plan:
3. Please list the site(s) and physical location(s) where students will participate in virtual mentoring sessions.	
4. How many mentors will use virtual mentoring in your program?	
5. Have you secured or do you need to secure permission from any school sites or other organizations to conduct virtual mentoring? Please explain.	
6. Describe how you will ensure that the technology requirements for virtual mentoring are met (i.e., students and mentors have access to the following software and hardware elements: computer or connected device, microphone, headphones, and GoBoard.com account).	
7. Describe how supervision will be maintained during all virtual mentoring sessions by TSIC staff or school liaisons (i.e., how will your program ensure that the mentoring location is a "safe space"?).	
8. Please describe how you will identify students and mentors who will use virtual mentoring. If you have a specific list of participants, please attach it.	
9. Please indicate the planned launch date for your implementation of virtual mentoring.	
10. Do you anticipate any challenges with launching virtual mentoring? If so, what are they and how will you address them?	

ATTACHMENT B:

Samples from the TSIC Mentor Toolkit

The following five activities are excerpts from the TSIC Mentor Toolkit that have been identified as appropriate for use with virtual mentoring. To access the TSIC Mentor Toolkit in its entirety, please go to www.tsic.org.

The included excerpts are:

- Activity 1 – A Few of My Favorite Things
- Activity 2 – I Have S.M.A.R.T. Goals
- Activity 3 – What Makes Me Tick
- Activity 4 – The Trick to Note-Taking
- Activity 5 – Test Time!

ACTIVITY 1: A FEW OF MY FAVORITE THINGS

Learning Objective: The mentor and mentee will become more familiar with each other by learning about personal preferences. The mentor and mentee will identify commonalities in their preferences and opinions.

Materials: "A Few of My Favorite Things" worksheet, pencils/pens.

Instructions: Prior to beginning the session, provide your mentee with a copy of this worksheet. Ask the mentee to take ten minutes to write their responses to each "favorite." You should plan to do the same. During your session, compare notes. How are your responses similar? Where do they differ? As you compare, try to identify at least a few commonalities. When possible, ask your mentee to provide further context to their response ("Why do you like X?").

A Few of My Favorite Things	
Book	
Song	
Movie	
TV Show	
Color	
Season	
Celebrity	
Place To Be	
Hobby	
Food	
Website	
Sport or Game	
Animal	

Finding common ground will help strengthen your relationship with your mentee. Based on the preferences and similarities identify, work together to plan out the perfect shared day: Where would you go? What activities would you take part in? What food would you eat? What music would you listen to? What season would it be?

ACTIVITY 2: I HAVE S.M.A.R.T. GOALS

Learning Objective: The mentees will set reasonable and attainable goals for different aspects of their lives.

Materials: "My S.M.A.R.T. Goal" worksheet, pencils or pens.

Instructions: Use the worksheet below to talk through a sample goal in one aspect of your own life (academic, career, or personal). Then work together to craft a goal for your mentee's life, letting them choose the achievement they would like to work on. Discuss a plan to periodically check in with each other on your goals. If one goal is completed, use this format to create an action plan for achieving another!

My S.M.A.R.T. Goals

My Goal: _____

Type of Goal (check one): Academic _____ Career_____ Personal_____

Specific (Who, What,When): _____

Measurable (How much/many):_____

Achievable (Steps I will take to achieve): _____

Relevant (Important because): _____

Timely (I will achieve by):_____

ACTIVITY 3: WHAT MAKES ME TICK

Learning Objective:

The student will explore personal values, interests, and experiences.

Instructions: Read the phrases aloud and ask your student to orally complete them with the first idea that comes to mind.

> ➢ If I had a week-long vacation, I would . . .

> ➢ On weekends, I wish my family would . . .

> ➢ If I had $10, I would . . .

> ➢ I think my parents should . . .

> ➢ The thing that scares me the most is . . .

> ➢ People I like always . . .

> ➢ I cry when . . .

> ➢ I am afraid to . . .

> ➢ I am happy when . . .

> ➢ I am proud that I . . .

> ➢ When I grow up, I want to be . . .

> ➢ In my spare time, I like to . . .

> ➢ The most important quality in a family is . . .

> ➢ I like people who . . .

> ➢ Five years from now, I would like to . . .

> ➢ I would like to travel to . . .

> ➢ I would like to make a difference in the world by . . .

- ➢ I am really good at . . .

- ➢ I get angry when . . .

- ➢ My friends think I am . . .

- ➢ I am loneliest when . . .

- ➢ In school, I do my best when . . .

- ➢ I feel the most love when . . .

Choose a response to a phrase discussed above that caught your attention, and encourage your student to elaborate on his or her answer. Share your answers as well, identifying where you have felt similar or had similar experiences and how you chose to handle it.

ACTIVITY 4: THE TRICK TO NOTE-TAKING

Learning Objective:

The student will evaluate their note-taking habits and review some note-taking tips.

Instructions:

Effective note-taking is important for students to retain information learned in class. Use the discussion questions below to determine whether your student is taking effective notes.

Use the tips below to help your student improve their note-taking habits.

> Do you review and edit your notes within 24 hours after each of your classes?
>
> Do you try to write down everything your teacher says?
>
> Are you able to understand your notes when you study for a test?
>
> Do you tend to miss a lot of information when you take notes?
>
> Do you read ahead in your textbooks?

Be selective. Avoid trying to write down every word or writing in complete sentences.

Abbreviate. Reduce common words/phrases to symbols and eliminate connecting words like: is, are, was, the, and would. Drop the last few letters of words, e.g., write "approx" for "approximately." Try using "formula" statements to take notes. For example, the teacher says, "The diameter of the earth is four times greater than the diameter of the moon." You write, "Earth=4x>diameter of moon."

Focus on the main points. Use "significance" statements. Identify the main concepts and state why they are important. If the information being given is important, a speaker will usually do one of the following: pause before or after an idea, use repetition to emphasize a point, or write an idea on the board.

Identify significance. Ask yourself, is the information being discussed new or is it covered in the text? You can do this by looking over the class assignment prior to class. To be successful, make sure you are a step ahead and have a working knowledge of the topic.

Ask questions. Make sure you clarify areas that are unclear or confusing.

Reference examples. Concrete examples are often the best way to clarify complex ideas.

Review notes ASAP. The sooner you review your notes, the better you retain the information.

ACTIVITY 5: TEST TIME!

Learning Objective:

The student will become familiar with different types of test-taking strategies to use when studying.

Instructions:

There are many different types of tests: essays, true/false, and multiple-choice, to name a few. Knowing how to study for them can help your mentee sharpen their test-taking skills. During your session, review the various test preparation tips. Work together to create an action plan for preparing for their next test.

General test prep tips:

Concentrate on learning what you do not know

- Ask your teacher for help, if necessary
- Anticipate the questions
- Create a study outline
- Ask questions
- Make a study schedule

Essay Tests

Keep Track of Your Time If you have five questions to answer in 40 minutes, for example, make sure you do not spend too much time on any one question.

Read Through the Questions Once By familiarizing yourself with all the questions first, you will have much more time to consider your answers.

Identify and Circle the Directive Words Read the directions carefully and pinpoint the key terms. If a teacher wants you to describe, then do so; if she wants you to evaluate, then do not worry so much about description.

Outline Your Answer First Teachers are greatly influenced by the coherence and structure of your answer. To list facts in random order makes it seem as if you do not have a clear grasp of the material. Try to organize your answers as well as you can.

Take Time to Write an Introduction and Conclusion A strong introduction and conclusion are essential parts of a good essay. They give your responses the structure of logical arguments.

True/False Tests

- Look for any word in the question that could make it false.
- Look out for extreme modifiers that tend to make a question false: all, none, never, only, etc.
- Identify qualifiers that tend to make questions true: usually, frequently, often, probably, etc.

Multiple-Choice Tests

- Read each question with the intention of answering without looking at the possible answers.
- Use educated guessing: Eliminate two choices quickly and then decide between the remaining two.
- Choose the numbers in the middle range, not the extremes, when guessing.
- When in doubt, choose answers that are longer and more descriptive.
- When two similar answers appear, one is likely correct.

Take Stock in
Children®

For additional mentor resources and to access
an electronic version of the Mentor Toolkit,
please visit our website at:
www.takestockinchildren.org/toolkit